B M

Mark and Me

Mark McGwire and the Truth Behind Baseball's Worst-Kept Secret

Jay McGwire

TRIUMPH
BOOKS

Triumph Books and colophon are registered trademarks of Random House, Inc.

Library of Congress Cataloging-in-Publication Data

McGwire, Jay.
  Mark and me : Mark McGwire and the truth behind baseball's worst-kept secret / Jay McGwire.
    p. cm.
  ISBN 978-1-60078-308-1
  1. McGwire, Mark, 1963– 2. Baseball players—United States—Biography.
3. McGwire, Jay. 4. Brothers—United States—Biography. I. Title.
  GV865.M396A3 2010
  796.357092—dc22
  [B]
                                    2009048981

This book is available in quantity at special discounts for your group or organization. For further information, contact:

Triumph Books
542 South Dearborn Street
Suite 750
Chicago, Illinois 60605
(312) 939-3330
Fax (312) 663-3557
www.triumphbooks.com

Printed in U.S.A.
ISBN: 978-1-60078-308-1

Design by Patricia Frey
All photos courtesy of the author except insert pages 7 and 8 (top).

Mark McGwire is my brother,
and I know the truth.

This is our story.

Contents

chapter | one

The Beginning

From an early age, people knew that Mark was going to be special. When I went to the ballpark or school, I was a somebody just being his brother.

Kid brothers are supposed to look up to their older brothers, and I'm no exception. The fact is I adore all four of my older brothers. Mark just happens to be the icon of the bunch.

We grew up in Southern California on a sleepy little cul-de-sac in idyllic Claremont. My father worked as a dentist, and my mother groomed five young boys with fair skin and straight white teeth—after braces—to be champion athletes.

Anyone who knew my father wouldn't have been surprised at the resolve, direction, and patience he had for leading his boys on a path he could not take for himself. In 1944, at age seven, Dad was diagnosed with poliomyelitis in his right leg. He was sent to a contagious-patients ward at a Spokane, Washington, hospital. It would be another 10 years before a polio vaccine would be available.

I have imagined being in his shoes—a child alone in a hospital room where even his parents weren't allowed because the doctors didn't know if his disease was transmittable. All he could do was wave through a window to his parents standing outside. I can't imagine how scared he was. He must have wondered, why him, and if he would ever be able to be a normal kid. Well, he didn't let polio beat him then, and he hasn't let it beat him since.

His leg was shortened and has atrophied due to the effects of polio. It's almost skin on bone. He needs to wear a platform shoe to balance his stride. But he has never given in to the disabling effects of the disease.

Dad had a love of athletics, and I think he probably appreciated them more because of his own physical limitations. He didn't play competitive sports growing up, though he did enjoy playing around. He boxed a little, and friends have said he could throw a football 70 yards on one leg. Playing basketball, he'd stand underneath the hoop and wait for someone to pass the ball so that he could lay it up for a score. He had a lifelong love of golf and routinely walked 18 holes with an eight handicap. My dad was nothing short of remarkable.

He met my mother while attending dental school at the University of Washington. Like Dad, she loved sports. She played softball, basketball, anything she could. Back then, there weren't as many opportunities; women's sports were nowhere near as varied as they are today.

My parents married in a Catholic church in 1960. Two years later they had their first child, Michael. Shortly thereafter they moved to Pomona, California, where Dad set up a general dentistry practice. When Mark was born in 1963, their small house in Pomona grew smaller. Next came my brother Bob, followed by Dan.

When I was born in 1970, it prompted a move to tonier Claremont and a 4,000-square-foot house on a cul-de-sac on Siena Court. Our home had three bedrooms and two bathrooms upstairs, with the master bedroom on the main floor. I can't blame them wanting to have peace and quiet away from us. Mike, the eldest, had his own room; I shared a room with Dan, and Mark and Bob teamed up. As my brothers grew up and left the house, we shifted around and spread out.

The wheels of the McGwire sports factory had already begun to turn by the time I came. With five boys in the house, my parents viewed sports as an outlet for the kids to work out their energy and thus an avenue for their own sanity. Our neighborhood facilitated that. Kids played in the streets and rode their bicycles everywhere. It was *Ozzie and Harriet, Leave It to Beaver,* and *Happy Days* all rolled into one. My parents were a young couple in a neighborhood full of them. They made a lot of friends, and everyone's kids played together. It seemed like there was a barbecue every weekend. Our universe consisted of spending time with the family, hanging out in the garage, and playing football out front with the neighborhood kids.

As the youngest, everybody made me feel like I was a special treasure. My brothers would pick me up and hug me like they might a family pet. People would dote on me and called me "Baby John." (I've had a number of nicknames throughout my life—John John, JJ, Little Mac—after my brother Mark, "Big Mac"—and Jay, as I'm still known today.)

When I rode my Big Wheel around in the front yard, one of my brothers was always there, almost like a presidential escort. It couldn't have been a safer childhood. I had four older brothers and two wonderful parents. I was never isolated or left alone, and I believe that my dad ensured that his sons had what he didn't. Dad was an only child and isolated because of his illness. He spent most of his childhood alone until his parents remarried and half-siblings came along.

Dad has retired from his practice, but he still works at a clinic for the poor once a week. Over 40 years of practice, he established a huge following of patients on an impeccable reputation of kindness. He went out of his way for his patients and showed them a great deal of care—and they loved him for that. His sense of humor and generosity complemented his professional and meticulous manner and put his patients at ease. Nobody likes to get his teeth worked on, but I think going to the dentist was a lot easier with my father in the chair. I always felt so proud when I visited my dad in his office and saw him work.

Despite his polio and the withered right leg—not to mention that his job required him to repeatedly get up and down from his dental stool—Dad did not start wearing a brace until he was about 60. He missed just one day of work in 40-plus years.

Dad became a cycling enthusiast and rode his bike everywhere. Once he even completed a 400-mile ride from San Francisco to Santa Barbara. For many years he rode the bike for exercise, basically with his one good leg. After a ride he would return home and hit the heavy bag and speed bag, which he had set up in the garage. He's a tough dude both physically and mentally. I think we McGwire boys all got that from him.

We never looked at my dad as if there was something wrong with him, and he kept up with everyone. He made no excuses for his disability. Instead, we saw how hard he worked and strove to be that way ourselves. I think that is why all of us have been successful in our own ways—we've all gone after it.

My mother is the backbone of our family. She is tireless and full of energy. She turned out to be quite a fighter herself, surviving melanoma. She went to the cancer unit when I was five years old, and out of all the people there, she was the only survivor. I thank God for saving my mom. I can't imagine life without her. She was always there for the big things and the small ones. And her survival instincts were not lost on us. Our parents' message was clear to each of us: No obstacle can stop us.

While we inherited our drive from our parents, we also got their size. Dad stands 6'4" and Mom 5'10". At church, our family took up a full pew sitting shoulder to shoulder. Three of my brothers are redheaded, Dan and I have strawberry-blonde hair, and all of us are fair skinned. We were your typical Irish brood, only bigger.

I don't know how my parents managed to feed five giants. When we sat down to eat, it was an extreme sport, and whoever ate the most in 20 minutes won. Mom cooked us three square meals a day, and every one was a smorgasbord. We grew up on meat and potatoes, and we loved loading up on beef stroganoff, chicken tetrazzini, and homemade pizza. When Mom made pancakes in the morning, she made enough batter to feed an army. We all had huge appetites. My parents would spend $200 to $300 a week on food, a lot of money in the late 1970s and long before the days of Sam's Club or Costco. My friends were wide-eyed over how much food we had in the pantry. They loved to come over and see what kind of food we had around. We had two large refrigerators, one in the house and one in the garage, which were always filled to the brim, and a huge freezer in the garage. We grew and grew, all of us tall and skinny, like a family of basketball players.

Dad taught all of us to golf. He encouraged us to get involved in athletics and served as the head coach of our baseball and soccer teams for a number of years. He could always be counted on to show us the right way to do things, like how to properly grip a golf club. He's a practical, patient guy. As a kid, golf was boring to me—slow and hard to get that ball to go straight. I became frustrated, so I never really pursued it. But my brothers were good, and they still play today. They all shoot in the 70s and 80s, but Mark is the best of the bunch, a scratch golfer. I have to really play well to shoot in the 80s today, but I have a natural swing because of the mechanics my dad taught me as a kid.

My parents didn't know much about soccer, but they encouraged all of us to join teams. It was our first and favorite sport—baseball came along later. And as always, my dad was the coach.

As the youngest, I watched my brothers play and excel in all sports before me. Every one of them was exceptional. Funny enough, Mark hit a home run in his first-ever Little League at-bat. Even so, I think Dan was the best in Little League. He had an incredibly strong arm and pitched so hard that he struck everybody out. We all played for the Athletics of the Claremont Little League. We wore a uniform similar to the one that Mark would wear in his major league seasons with the Oakland Athletics, although our shirts were double-knit and our white pants resembled support hose.

True to his nature, Dad coached by encouragement, unlike many of the parents whose unattractive sides came out on the bleachers. My dad was always calm. If we lost a big game, he was always there with a "we'll get 'em next time." More than anything, he let us kids play the game. He was instructive, but he didn't stuff the game down our throats. He just let us have fun.

Claremont Little League felt like home in those years. I ate a lot of lunches and dinners at the concession stand. And I did spend a lot of my time there watching one or more of my brothers play. I might have been playing catch off to the side with one of my friends during the games, but when I heard one of my brothers' names announced, I always stopped to watch their at-bats. Mark, Bob, and Dan all hit a lot of home runs in Little League. I loved going to the park and watching them hit that ball until it disappeared. The sound an aluminum bat made when they swung just resonated differently. I felt so proud to have brothers who dominated.

From an early age, people knew that Mark was going to be special. It didn't matter the sport—whenever he played, he made the difference. When I went to the ballpark or school, I was a somebody just being his brother.

Of course my brothers' on-field successes fueled my desire to do as well as they did. I tried to mimic what they did to get the same results. In our house, we excelled in sports—that's just what McGwires did. We were a family to be reckoned with. We were the McGwires of the Claremont Little League A's. Everybody knew how good we were. And it wasn't just baseball, either. We played soccer, basketball, and flag football.

But our family wasn't well-known just because we were good athletes. It was also because my parents were so well liked. They hosted pool parties and the end-of-the-season team parties. They were fun, outgoing, and gracious hosts. They got along with anybody, and everybody loved them. Our house was always full of people

We spent our time outside playing over the line, kill the guy with the ball, hide and seek, ding dong ditch, Wiffle ball, handball, soccer, Nerf football, basketball…any competition we could think of. We played Marco Polo and Nerf baseball, and inevitably the ball would get hit on top of our roof or over the fence. We also had an AstroTurf putting green in the backyard next to a Ping-Pong table on which we played tournaments day or night. On the rare days it rained, we played Nerf basketball inside or Intellivision on the TV. After dinner, we'd beg to go back outside, and we played under the streetlights until it was time to go to bed. Whether we were playing on organized teams or just goofing around with friends, we always found a way to compete.

There were no epic battles between me and my brothers, just the usual competitive stuff. In basketball games, my older brothers just stuffed me. They never let me beat them. They always said, "We don't care if you're younger. We don't feel sorry for you, and we're not going to let you win." And I didn't. But it did help turn me into a great athlete.

I was the baby of the family, but that didn't keep them from giving me charley horses, a nipple twister, or some big-time wedgies. My brothers viewed me as spoiled because I was the youngest. But I always felt like they loved me and wanted the best for me.

I never felt any pressure to be good at sports despite the successes of my brothers. I just sort of followed their lead. Sports were something I wanted to do because I wanted to be just as good as my brothers. I banked everything I'd learned from playing sports with them and their friends to become a dominating figure on the local sports scene. All of it felt preordained.

I didn't have a favorite sport. I played soccer, basketball, baseball, and football—and I liked them all. I knew I was good though from the time I started playing T-ball, because the coach would pitch to you, and if you missed it, they put it on a tee. Well, I hit it over everyone's head.

My brothers taught me how to play soccer and to kick with my left foot. I averaged four or five goals a game. I played against my bigger brothers all the time and lost to them, but when I went out there on the field with kids my own age, they just couldn't compete. When I played sports, having my brothers there to watch me meant everything to me. My brothers each maintained that they worked the hardest with me because I was the youngest, and they felt my success was their success.

Everybody wanted to be on my team at recess. I would pick people who weren't so good so that I could help them out just liked my brothers did with me. I knew how it felt to get beat up in sports by people who are bigger and better than you. I hit the ball farther and I threw it faster than anybody else. Once, playing dodgeball, my teacher told me to calm down because I was throwing so hard.

Everything rolled along fine for me except school, where I always struggled. I consistently had to work harder in school to keep my grades up. It only made me want to focus more on sports.

chapter | two

The Hero

I lived vicariously through Mark, imagining the day when it would be my turn.

It wasn't until high school that Mark's exceptional talent really got him noticed.

Our brother Mike played golf and soccer growing up and was good at both, but he didn't have the desire to continue in sports like the other boys did. Mike was the scholar of the family. By his senior year, he was most often reading, doing Bible study, and listening to praise music. Looking back, Mike planted those first seeds of Christ in my heart without me knowing it at the time. (It would turn out to be a blessing later in my life.) My dad loves reading and encouraged all of us to do the same. But what kid likes to read? Mike and Dan were the only brothers who really followed in Dad's footsteps in that respect. Both of them went on to earn college degrees.

Every kid should have an older brother like Mike. He had a big influence on me. Mike took me running and hiking with him, and we also listened to Christian music together. To me, it seemed like he always made the right decisions and did the right things. He was a huge role model growing up.

Mike got the first car of all the brothers, a hand-me-down from Dad. When Mark got his driver's license, he shared the car with Mike—a 1967 Mustang. Later, Bob became the mechanic for the family. He has always been great with his hands and loves working on cars.

The stereotypical view of Southern California is one of laid-back surfer dudes who couldn't care less about other sports. Far from it. Where we lived, the sports were hypercompetitive. Every team was filled with kids clamoring to play football, baseball, basketball, or soccer.

Mark began high school at Claremont High, which Mike attended, but he decided after his first semester to transfer to rival Damien High, a private Catholic school 15 minutes away from our home. Claremont and Damien were fierce rivals in every sport. Whenever they met, the stands were jam-packed with people wearing Damien's green and yellow and

Claremont's white and maroon. Mark's transfer wasn't a big deal at the time because he was still young and hadn't established himself as a first-class athlete yet. If the coaches at Claremont had any inkling of the kind of athlete Mark would turn out to be, there might have been a bigger fuss about the whole thing. For some reason, Mark just didn't like Claremont, and he told my parents so. He wanted to be at a school where he felt they took their sports more seriously, and my parents supported his decision. Damien had a good reputation for sports at that time. They were really competitive in every sport and had good coaches, especially the head baseball coach Tom Carroll.

It was at Damien that Mark really started on fire. He was totally devoted to organized sports, particularly baseball and basketball but also golf for a time. His size and technique were impressive. By the time he started his junior year in high school, he stood 6'5", but he was a string bean of a redheaded kid. Everybody called him "Tree."

Mark was a student of his sports, continually striving for excellence. His intellectual dedication played an integral role in his success. Not only was he extremely coachable, absorbing all the right stuff, he also understood the proper techniques and mechanics required for success, whether it was how to box out his man, grab a rebound, or grip a baseball. Some people never grasp those sorts of mechanics. Mark just had a natural feel for how to play any game and a laser focus. He's always been that way—able to give something his undivided attention. Put simply, he was the sort of athlete you wanted on your team.

During Mark's sophomore year, he temporarily quit the baseball team to focus on golf, justifying his decision with the rationale that the only person to blame for anything that went wrong on the golf course was you. But the hiatus was brief, and he was back to baseball in short order.

Mark had just a couple of close friends in high school, though he knew a lot of people because of sports. Damien was an all-boys high school, so there weren't any girls around. He was pretty much a straight-laced guy and a late bloomer when it came to girls. He remained a dedicated athlete and stayed focused on those goals.

Mark is six-and-a-half years older than me, and I lived vicariously through what he did, imagining the day when it would be my turn. I loved watching him play any sport but particularly basketball. The speed of basketball held my interest more than the slower pace of some other sports.

Mark played center. He had a nice shot and could pretty much scoop up anything underneath the basket. He wasn't one of these guys you see doing acrobatic dunks and making all kinds of shots; he was a solid and physical player who played with real grit. Nobody could really push him around. Dan ended up being the real basketball star of the family—and he had real game!—but as a 10-year-old kid, watching Mark play was my first exposure to big-time high school sports, and I found the experience exhilarating.

My brothers always let me tag along to their games, particularly to Mark's. Being inside a real basketball gym really got me jazzed. I loved everything about the basketball court, from the sound of a leather ball bouncing on a wooden floor to the squeaking of sneakers when the players were really grinding on defense. I think I became a pretty good basketball player because I had spent so much time in that environment. Just being around a sport makes you better—you can't help but pick things up. I really do believe that a big part of my success came from me watching my brothers. I was the kid always tagging along. My real name is John Joseph McGwire, and everybody called me "JJ." And I loved to hear them say it—"There's little JJ."

Sometimes Mark drove me to the gym with him, and I'd bring the basketball with me to occupy the idle time. If the team used up all of the space inside the gym during practice or a game, I went outside to shoot hoops. All the other kids whose brothers were on the team would be outside playing, too. It was like a second family. Everyone went to see his or her brother play ball, and that's how you made other friends. For a kid like me who was obsessed with sports, this was heaven.

Eventually it became clear that Mark's best sport was baseball—only everyone thought he would reach the majors on the mound. He could flat-out throw a baseball. As tall as he was, when he pushed off the rubber toward home, he created a steep angle with his pitches that made him wicked to hit.

After his junior year, he began to work with Frank Pastore, a major league pitcher. The Cincinnati Reds had picked Pastore as the second pick of the 1975 draft. He went on to pitch eight seasons in the major leagues, six of them with the Reds, ending his career with the Minnesota Twins. Pastore stood 6'3", so he knew a little bit about the mechanics of pitching as a tall person. Pastore's in-laws, the Pignotis, were friends with our family and lived in nearby Upland. Being under Pastore's wing helped Mark smooth out some of the rough spots. Mark developed a better understanding of his own mechanics while learning some of the subtler nuances of pitching.

By the time Mark reached his senior season, he was throwing in the low 90s. Scouts sat in the stands with their radar guns clocking his fastball. And he could hit with power, too. People still talk about some of the home runs Mark hit in high school. They remain a basis of comparison. It's not uncommon to hear people say, "So-and-so might have hit that ball well, but when Mark McGwire played around here, he hit a ball way over there." He had bulked up to over 200 pounds by then, and when anyone that size—anyone who knows what he's doing—gets a hold of a ball, it's going to go a long way—particularly with an aluminum bat.

Imagine Mark hitting with an aluminum bat. Scary, isn't it? In my young eyes, Mark's heroics in athletics were Herculean feats. But I do know that his promise was evident, and that's why everybody was interested in him.

All of the local papers wrote about Mark, how he would get a college scholarship or get drafted by a major league team. To his credit, he never got an inflated ego. He continued to be just Mark, which included looking after his kid brother. He took time to pass on his baseball knowledge to me, teaching me the finer points of hitting and pitching, such as how to hold the seams of the ball, how to hold a curve ball, or how to throw a change-up without giving away that you're throwing a change-up. I developed a really nice change-up that looked like a fastball on release. I had a lot of innate advantages, but the instruction I got from Mark put me on another level in Little League. I struck out a lot of kids, and I could hit really well.

Those were exciting days. Mark was a success, and I was just beginning to understand how good I was in my own right. My brothers were starting to notice, too. I was tall and quick. I might have been young, but I understood that being lean, strong, and fast would help my athletic pursuits. And I was better earlier than my brothers. Whatever sport I played, I played it well. Everything my brothers had taught me, everything I had acquired from competing against them, the athletic skills and the toughness, all began to pay off for me. I could see my future in sports. I just knew I would be a professional athlete. The only question was, in which sport?

Despite Mark's obvious power potential, the Montreal Expos drafted him as a pitcher in the eighth round of the 1981 draft. Rod Dedeaux also wanted Mark to pitch at the University of Southern California. Everybody considered the USC coach a living legend.

Dedeaux began coaching the Trojans in 1942, but then he entered the Navy. When Dedeaux returned from military service, he assumed a role as a co-head coach, and the Trojans won the College World Series in 1948. In 1950, he became USC's only coach, and the Trojans turned into a power-house. A cool piece of trivia about Dedeaux that most people do not know: he worked for a dollar a year. He had a successful trucking business that allowed him to pursue his passion of coaching college baseball without having to worry about money. A look at the list of players who played for him is astounding: Ron Fairly, Tom Seaver, Dave Kingman, Don Buford, Roy Smalley, and Fred Lynn, just to name a few.

Mark had the option of signing with the Expos for $8,500 or attending USC on a baseball scholarship, and he went with USC. My parents were really proud that their son chose college. To this day, I don't know why Mark didn't sign with the Expos. Maybe he didn't feel he was polished enough to begin professional baseball. Certainly the prospect of playing for Dedeaux was compelling. So he headed to Los Angeles to pitch for the Trojans.

Meanwhile, Mike was at the University of San Diego, from which he graduated. He's been in school most of his life. He's received two PhDs, a master's degree, and a business degree. Of all the brothers, Mike is our undisputed scholar.

Mike's departure for college didn't feel that strange. Looking back, I find that strange. But I guess when he left, we all accepted it as part of the natural progression: you finish high school and head off to college. Plus, as busy as we all were playing sports, we kind of put his being away out of our minds. I think it was the same for Mark, too. Even though the two of them were close in age, they had gone to different high schools and had different friends and interests.

In 1983, a couple of years after Mark, Bob graduated from Damien. A year later he moved out and got married, leaving Dan and me as the two remaining McGwire brothers in our once-boisterous home.

chapter | three

The Evolution

Neither Mark nor Dan had been turned on to the benefits of weight training, but I was getting really serious about it. In my mind, it was the "extra something" that would take me further than them.

Mark's acceptance to USC was a big deal in our family. We were all very proud of him. And attending the games he played became a regular family outing. It wasn't a big ordeal to get there since we only lived about 40 minutes away. Typically my parents let me invite a few friends, and we'd all drive down together. Those trips were a lot of fun, and I was always excited to go. There I was, a 12-year-old kid, and my brother was playing for a major university. If he did well, I knew I could read about it in the *Los Angeles Times*. He wasn't just on the team at USC, either—he was one of the star players! It made a huge impression on me.

Usually we would arrive early, and Mark would take me inside the Rod Dedeaux complex and into the locker room to hang with the guys. The Los Angeles Dodgers' manager, Tommy Lasorda, and Coach Dedeaux were close friends, and the walls were lined with pictures of the two of them mugging together alongside photographs of the different USC players who had gone on to the major leagues. Just looking at those pictures could make anyone want to be a major leaguer. I thought Mark had it made.

The players' weight room on campus was like nothing I'd ever seen before. Talk about all the bells and whistles! Every piece of equipment was state of the art. The whole place sparkled to me. My eyes grew wide at that weight room. It was love at first sight. I could only dream about being able to inhabit such a grand place. Mark wasn't much into lifting weights back then, as the prevailing baseball mentality stated that weight lifting would ruin your swing—as if you couldn't catch up to a fastball with bulging biceps. (Of course, that would be proven wrong in the years that followed.)

I might have been young, but I already had fallen for the strongman look. *The Incredible Hulk* was a huge sensation in 1977, and its star, professional bodybuilder Lou Ferrigno, was magnetic. I just loved that show. Something captured me about the way the Hulk dominated everybody because of his strength and size. I was under no delusions about getting as huge as the Hulk someday, but I did want to become a strongman, most definitely.

I was already aware that I possessed the gift of strength. In elementary school I could do way more push-ups and sit-ups than anybody else. And the weird thing was, I liked doing them, while nobody else did. I had a boundless energy, and the motivation to become bigger, faster, and stronger. Perhaps that's just the McGwire way, but I always wanted to exert myself physically.

My brother Bob and I started lifting weights around the same time; he was a senior in high school by then, and I was 13. We set up a makeshift weight room in the garage where we pumped iron. We had a set of those round plastic weights filled with cement, the kind you could get at Sears or any sporting goods store. Every kid I knew had a set, though most never touched them. Bob and I used them so much that the cement crumbled inside because of the way we treated them, constantly dropping the weights on the floor. Dad lifted weights a little bit, too, though he concentrated mostly on his hundred-pound bag and the speed bag.

It was during those days spent in the garage that a weight lifter was born in me. We lifted two or three times a week, on average. Did we have any idea how to lift properly? Well, no. But we did the basics: bench press, squats, biceps curls, triceps presses. We started reading muscle magazines and learned more as we went along.

I loved those magazines. Even back then I loved working my legs. It is the toughest workout of all the body parts, and making strides with one's legs takes a huge amount of effort to accomplish. Most people don't like it because it hurts so much. But I found that burn and that pump exhilarating. And the physical pain reminded me of my own success. Every gain made was directly proportional to the amount of effort put in. Reaching a point where my muscles burned and getting my heart rate pumping through the roof helped me burn all my energy off. After lifting for just a short time, all of that physical exertion kind of mellowed me out. It definitely quashed a lot of the hyperactivity I had at that age. Unwittingly, I had discovered a path to inner peace, my own state of nirvana—even if that peace lasted only as long as my latest pump. And anticipating the effect that work would have on my body only made things better.

One could say my eyes were opened wide, looking around in that weight room at USC. Having all that at my disposal would be one of the best trimmings to have as an athlete. I could see my future. And I resolved that nothing would stop me from reaching my goal.

Mark understood my goals and saw how much I looked up to him. Whenever we went to see him play, he couldn't have treated me any better. Everyone on the team made me feel welcome, a tribute to the fact that they all liked him. After a while, I felt like I was a part of the team in some small way. I met Jack Del Rio, who played catcher for USC and went on to success as a football player and as head coach of the Jacksonville Jaguars. I also met a stringbean pitcher named Randy Johnson, who would go on to become one of the most dominant pitchers in the game, winning five Cy Youngs and garnering 10 All-Star nods. Mark even arranged for me to go out on the field with the team and play catch with him and some of the guys. The first time I went out onto that field I was awestruck. The grass was as pristine as the fairways at Pebble Beach, and the clay wasn't the hard stuff I was used to from Little League. To me, it was the closest thing to the big leagues without being in the big leagues. And Mark was turning into some kind of latter-day Babe Ruth—the pitcher who became a hitter.

During Mark's freshman year, he put up pretty solid numbers on the mound, going 4–4 with a 3.04 ERA. He also played nine games in positions other than pitcher and hit .200 with three home runs and 11 RBIs in 75 at-bats. Even though the numbers weren't great, Mark showed power potential. It was enough to make the Trojan coaching staff think about how well he might do as an everyday player.

In the summer after his freshman season, USC received a request from the Anchorage Glacier Pilots of the Alaska Summer League to help them fill a roster spot. The league is a well-respected tool for college teams, a summertime league in which youngsters are groomed during the off-season. Ron Vaughn, who was an assistant for the Pilots as well as an assistant coach for USC, suggested Mark. So off my brother went to Alaska.

It was his first summer away from home, and he struggled a little bit, I think. Apart from being a little homesick, the Pilots shuffled him to first base. Jim Dietz, who coached at San Diego State, was Mark's coach in Alaska. He sensed Mark battling through the position change, so he began to chat up Ruth's story. He also reminded him about Dave Kingman, a pitcher at USC who became a major league position player and a feared slugger. Kingman, like Mark, had amazing power. Vaughn helped my brother with his mechanics by getting him to lower his hands and balance his stance, which resulted in a natural swing that simply crushed the baseball.

By the time Mark returned to classes in the fall, he had warmed to the idea of playing first base. His summer instruction paid immediate dividends as the Trojans' sophomore first baseman. The fact that he got to play every day as a first baseman, rather than waiting around for every fifth day as a pitcher, only sweetened the deal.

In his junior year he exploded, tying the school record for home runs with 32 in 67 games. It was a huge breakout that opened the eyes of scouts and fueled him with the confidence that he could take his game to the next level. I have often wondered if Mark would have found his way to the majors as a pitcher. I truly believe that recognizing Mark for his power with the bat was a huge blessing.

I recall a trip we took to Tempe, Arizona, to watch USC play Arizona State. The buildup felt like a championship fight: USC's Mark McGwire versus Arizona State's Barry Bonds. Bonds already had it all—and he was just a sophomore! He could run, hit for power, and hit for a high average. He was very obviously an all-around talent. And Mark cut the figure of the stereotypical slugging first baseman. Everybody talked about them and speculated about whether each would be drafted and how high. They both were, of course—Mark as the tenth overall pick in that June's draft by Oakland and Bonds as the sixth pick the following year, going to Pittsburgh. Ironically, both of them were ribbon thin, far from the hulking specimens they would later become.

Mark also began to blossom socially while at USC. The batgirl for the team, Kathy Hughes, became Mark's first serious girlfriend. Everybody loved her, my parents included. Mark and Kathy fell in love and got married in December of 1984.

*   *   *

Bob Baiz had coached Damien football when Mark was there, but he had moved to Claremont High by the time Dan got there in the early '80s. He and his family lived in our neighborhood. Their kids were the same age as us, and we had all played together around the neighborhood as well as countless poolside barbecues at the McGwire house. Their son, Louie, remains my brother Dan's good friend to this day.

Coach Baiz had seen Dan plays sports since Little League and knew he had an above-average arm. Then again, any good public-school coach should be able to identify the best talent in his area and anticipate how his team would come together as they came of age. He must have been licking his chops knowing that once Dan reached Claremont, he would have a slinging quarterback who could run his wide-open offense.

Dan was tall for a freshman and excelled in basketball and football. By the end of his sophomore year, he had surpassed Mark's height by a full two inches. He quit playing baseball after Colt League, despite the inherent advantages his height could provide him in pitching. Dan had the same leverage that Mark had, but he had a tougher time finding the strike zone. Two sports were plenty for him.

I just think the slow pace of baseball and its lack of pizzazz in comparison to basketball and football weighed in his decision. Dan played quarterback in football and center in basketball, two highly visible positions.

His choice was validated when, as a sophomore, he won the starting position on the varsity football team.

Mark was making it happen at USC, and Dan was doing special things right in front of me at Claremont. At the same time, I was excelling myself. I found success in Pony League, pitching well and hitting a lot of home runs. Once, Mark came to one of my games. I hit a home run that day, a real shot. And even Mark said, "No way, I can't believe how far that went!" I was beaming. Getting that confirmation from Mark and my other brothers convinced me that I would get there, too; at some point in the future I would reach the same heights.

Pursuing excellence in athletics occupied all my thoughts and time. My parents had held me back in first grade, and I had struggled as long as I can remember. I could study my brothers for the most-minute detail in order to improve my sports performance; I had to work exponentially harder just to get Bs and Cs in the classroom. I had trouble paying attention to class and often thought, *Who needs school?*

Neither Mark nor Dan had been turned on to the benefits of weight training, but I was getting really serious about it. In my mind, it was the "extra something" that would take me further than them. I considered it a high-enough plateau to catch up to Mark, but reaching the level of excellence that Dan had would really be a major achievement, I thought. Lifting would make me stronger, faster, and a better athlete; I just knew it. Nothing could stop me from finding a career in professional athletics; I had it all planned out. But as the old saying goes, "Want to make God laugh? Tell Him your plans."

It was the summer of 1984. Mark had just finished his junior year at USC when the Oakland A's drafted him. He signed a contract on July 20, 1984, that gave him a $125,000 signing bonus. That same summer, Mark played for the U.S. Olympic baseball team at the Summer Games in Los Angeles. He also played on the Pan-Am team that traveled to the Dominican Republic and Venezuela. He described it as complete culture shock—coming off of the plane to see army security with rifles and machine guns. The event drew almost 400,000 spectators, as eight teams from across the globe battled it out for the gold medal in the tournament. Team USA was being heralded as the country's best-ever amateur baseball team. In addition to Mark, the team featured Will Clark and Barry Larkin, both of whom went on to major league careers. Team USA went undefeated through round-robin play before beating Korea in the semifinals to earn a spot in the finals. They were upset 6–3 by Japan, a big underdog in the tournament. Mark only had four hits in 21 at-bats and no home runs. Even so, I do remember him showing an uncanny knack for doing splits at first base on close plays to nab the runner.

After the Olympics, Mark began his professional baseball career at Class-A Modesto of the California League. Former major leaguer George Mitterwald was the team's manager, and Mark joined them just in time to play in 16 games, hitting a dubious .200 and a single home run.

In 1985 he played his first full minor league season at Modesto. The team sported some future major leaguers in Charlie O'Brien, Mickey Tettleton, and Walt Weiss. The A's wanted to try him out as a third baseman, and that contributed to some of his growing pains. But he finished the 1985 season with a .274 batting average and a team-leading 24 home runs.

My parents let me visit him for a week that summer, and I was pumped. I was 15 years old, and Mark was my idol. All the fans at John Thurman Field in Modesto knew my brother and hounded him for his autograph, even back then. He was the organization's up-and-coming power hitter.

I went early to the yard with him every day and hung out with the players, just as I had with the USC team. Everybody called Mark "Big Mac," and in turn they called me "Little Mac." Mark carried a particular air about him, as if he was destined for greatness. My chest always swelled whenever someone said that he would make it to the major leagues. Anyone worth his salt could tell that he wouldn't stay in the minors for long.

I sat in the stands and watched the games with Kathy. She was a terrific lady who knew how to have fun. She and Mark lived in an apartment complex where a lot of the other players lived, too. Sure, it was the *minor league* life, but Mark had signed for a decent bonus. They seemed to be quite happy, both of them living through Mark's dream to become a major leaguer. Having been the batgirl during college, Kathy understood the baseball player's mentality. She wanted to do everything to help him achieve his goal.

During that trip, Mark and I hopped in his car to Oakland to see the A's play. Dave Kingman had 30 home runs for the A's that season and most of them were of the tape-measure variety. I think Mark enjoyed watching Kingman because there were so many parallels between their careers. Both played at USC, each had been a pitcher, Kingman initially had been a third baseman, and he hit epic bombs. I'll never forget that day. We had a great time at the game—who wouldn't want to spend a day at the ballpark with his big brother, himself a baseball star? It further crystallized the goal that I had for myself.

chapter | four

The Accident

*A lot of kids might have quit sports
after something like that. I didn't
want to give up. I felt that I owed
it to myself and my family.*

BB guns were the latest craze during my freshman year at Claremont High School. We lived well within walking distance to a canyon where the hills meet the San Bernardino Mountains. The canyon itself was filled with brush, but there were trails to walk along higher up on its slopes. I went up there a lot when I was younger—first with Mike, who had learned a lot about the outdoors as an Eagle Scout, such as how to recognize poison ivy, avoid snakes, determine direction…all sorts of useful things. Once I was a little older, my friends and I would go there to goof off. At its heights, it offered a spectacular view of the valley, our little world, below.

My friend Eric was really cool. His father was a black belt in kung fu. He also let him use BB guns and took him out shooting. Eric and I decided that we'd take the BB guns to the canyon to go shooting. At first we'd test our skills to see which one of us was the best shot. We shot at everything and anything—Coke cans, bottles, candy wrappers blowing by. You name it, we tried to pump it full of BBs. It became a regular activity. After a while, target practice got boring, so we decided to aim for each other instead. It wasn't physically dangerous; the pellets more or less bruised like a paintball. If you got hit, it would sting, but you would survive.

We had the kind of guns that you pump up with air, and the more you pumped the gun, the harder and faster the BB would travel. We always aimed below the waist and didn't pump the gun more than once or twice— that way if we got hit in the leg or something, we wouldn't be hurt. My parents disagreed.

My dad was firm: no shooting. He had heard about kids shooting guns in the canyon. He didn't know how often I'd been out there shooting, but he constantly warned me about playing with BB guns. It was the classic admonishment from the movie *A Christmas Story*: "You'll shoot your eye out."

So I lied. "I don't go up there," I assured him. "Don't worry about me, Dad."

But unbeknownst to him, my friend Eric's father had bought me a BB gun. I knew my dad wouldn't go for it—after all, his warnings echoed in my head—but I gladly accepted the gift and snuck around with it behind my father's back.

I have always been stubborn to a fault. I knew better than my parents. We all did—or so we thought. Then on Saturday afternoon in October 1985, six of us went up into the hills. My friend Jack Myers had spent the night at my house the night before and had been adamant about not wanting me to go shooting the next day. He was afraid that someone would get hurt. I gave him a hard time about not coming with us. Despite my goading, he was steadfast in his refusal.

I had just started my freshman year at Claremont High, and was the running back on the freshman football team. We were only a few games into the season, and already I was making a name for myself. I was tall for a running back, but I was fast and hit the line with power. I even had a few touchdowns under my belt. There was no football practice that Saturday, so I figured why not go shooting? I've got nothing better to do. The last thing on my mind was getting hurt.

We split up into two teams, with three guys on each team. I hid behind a tree, waiting for my target. The hills are really bushy, so the visibility wasn't great. I continued straining for a shot when all of a sudden something hit me in the eye. I was shocked, but it didn't feel real. It was almost as if I had imagined it had happened. There wasn't much pain. It was almost like a quick burst of pressure. I rubbed my right eye and looked down at my hand to see blood and tears. I wasn't sure what had happened or quite where I was hit. But I saw stars in that one eye, and my vision was dark and blurry.

So I closed my unaffected eye, and I couldn't see anything. That's when I called out to the other guys. Everybody thought I was joking, as if I was trying to decoy them to draw them out. It wasn't long before they figured out I wasn't kidding.

We walked to the nearest friend's house and called 911, and I was rushed to Pomona Valley Hospital. About an hour later the pain set in. My parents had been at church, and one of the priests had delivered the news to them. They arrived just in time to catch me in the ER before I went to surgery. Despite my disobedience, they didn't seem angry, just worried. We didn't know anything yet. I might never see again.

Pomona Valley is just a local hospital, and doctors there decided that the best course of action was to send me to specialists at the USC Medical Center. They had a doctor from Switzerland on their staff who was one of the best eye surgeons in the world. So they sewed up my eyelid and left the BB inside my eye—apparently the BB had pierced my eyelid and lodged in my eyeball—and suggested I get some rest before heading to USC.

Mark visited me the day after the accident. At that time we still weren't sure about the severity of the injury. But he understood what I didn't want to think about—the effect this might have on my athletic career—and he tried to keep my mind off things.

Time passed slowly while I waited to go to USC. I had a lot of time to be remorseful. I mean, come on, shooting BB guns at each other! Talk about dumb and dumber. Until this fateful trip, all of my trips to USC had promised to be happy ones, eagerly riding with my parents to the beautiful campus to watch Mark hit bombs.

The doctors would not know the extent of the damage until they pulled my eye out of its socket. It was a long few weeks before the surgery. They found the BB lodged in the back of my eye. It had come extremely close to hitting my brain and had destroyed my retina. Without a retina, you can't see. They were able to remove the BB and save the actual eye, but the retina could not be salvaged or reattached. I was blind in one eye.

I became a walking example for parents everywhere. Even worse, I went from being the McGwire with the most athletic potential to the McGwire with one eye. Overnight, everybody felt sorry for me, even my parents. My friends and football teammates visited me during my recovery. They signed a football for me and told me they'd see me next year. That felt good, but I was still sidelined from the sport that I loved.

During the months that followed I suffered a lot of pain in my eye socket. When it came, it was excruciating—it pulsed through my entire head. The whole year was an exercise in frustration. I had trouble adjusting to my new field of vision and often bumped into people and things.

I devoted myself, during those first six months, to making adjustments to recuperate from the change. Going back to school made me feel insecure. I worried about people's reactions—especially the girls'. I lacked confidence. I was depressed. I was filled with doubts about how I would ever overcome this. I could feel people's pity for me everywhere I went. I think that everyone who knew me understood what athletics meant to me, and they all assumed I'd never be able to play again. I disagreed. I knew I would play again; I just didn't know how good I could be. But I didn't want to let myself or my brothers down. I think they were proud of me for the way I went after it.

I was self-conscious about my appearance. My eye was shrunken from the impact, and it was constantly bloodshot. Later that year, I went to a cosmetic surgeon who specialized in eye injuries. He took an impression of my right eye and made a cosmetic shell to fit over it. He hand-painted the shell to match my other eye and balance the look. Today, a lot of people who meet me don't notice it; they don't know that I'm blind in my right eye.

Before the accident I had played basketball, baseball, and football. After the accident, I had to find ways to compensate for the loss of my eye. A lot of kids might have quit sports after something like that. I didn't want to give up. Knowing what Mom and Dad went through, I knew I couldn't. From them I had learned how to be a fighter. I felt that I owed it to myself and my family.

Up until that point, I had never been challenged by kids my own age. Now the playing field was leveled. I got clearance to participate and started playing basketball in my freshman year. I wore goggles to protect my good eye. So I had to find other ways to be competitive, and I did. Eventually I managed to put my ordeal in the rearview mirror, and it was as if nothing had happened.

It took a lot of love and support to get through it, but my family was there every step of the way. I don't know what would have happened to me if they hadn't been there.

Coming out of this, I realized how important my weight training had become to me. Working out gave me a boost in confidence that helped me overcome my diminished eyesight. My parents backed my zeal for weight training, likely as they saw the effect it had on my attitude. They wanted me to have something I could be passionate about.

That Christmas, they got me an Olympic weight set and changeable dumbbell set. It was the best Christmas present ever and a marked upgrade over the plastic and concrete weights I had been using. The weights were made of iron, and there was a bench and a cable pulley machine that could be converted into multiple exercise configurations.

Soon my friends noticed that I started to get bigger and wanted to work out with me. Even back then I knew how to push myself, and I pushed my friends just as hard. After the workouts we were so pumped up that if we tried to play a game of Horse in the driveway, no one would make a hoop. It was comical to watch. None of us had the touch with the basketball with our veins popping out and our muscles bulging.

I knew I would never give up pumping iron. I felt certain that I had found my life's passion, and it became my purpose and my salvation. I worked out four or five times a week, steadfast in my resolve to become the biggest and strongest. I also wanted to make the varsity football team my sophomore year.

I was living and breathing weight training. Violent Arnold Schwarzenegger movies such as *Conan the Barbarian* and *Commando* became my favorites. AC/DC, Van Halen, Metallica, and Guns 'n' Roses were my musical diet. It all fed into my attitude. I bought bodybuilding magazines to see how big Arnold was back in those days and every once in a while caught competitions like Mr. Olympia on television. I didn't know if I could ever make a living through bodybuilding; I just knew I wanted to be big and strong like those guys. I was motivated.

It's funny how one split second can affect a lifetime.

chapter | five

The Ascent

A lot of great things started happening
for our family all at once.

My world changed immeasurably after the accident that left me blind in one eye. Meanwhile, my brother Dan was on a roll.

When Mark left for USC, he was a local legend. Everybody in the area knew who he was, and there were plenty of stories about him, especially in baseball. He had set a high standard in athletics for us younger brothers to reach. My brother Dan didn't waste time thinking about surpassing Mark; he just did it. In high school, Dan took the McGwire name to another level, higher than Mark ever could have imagined.

Mark had been a blue-collar basketball player; Dan was a blue-chip athlete. Dan dunked over everybody whenever he took the basketball court, even guys much bigger than him. Compared to Mark, he just possessed a better sense of the game and his surroundings. He had Mark's toughness but more refined skills. He was an awesome talent, and his joy for the game was always evident.

Dan and his buddy Bobby Erpts frequently went to Laguna Beach and other beaches along the coastline to play pickup games. The Laguna Beach courts were built next to the sand, which made it easy for people to watch them play. A lot of guys went down there to play because there were always girls there enjoying the sun and the scene. Dan stood 6'8" and Bobby 6'9", and they dominated, dunking on everybody. Not only were they tall, but they played together seamlessly and understood each other's moves. That chemistry and their skills made them unbeatable.

As talented as Dan was in basketball, he might have been even better at football. I remember plenty of awe-inspiring plays during his high school career. As a quarterback, you have to be on top of things, because the quarterback is the guy who runs the engine of the team. Dan handled his Claremont team with incredible poise during the three years he stood behind center. And he performed with great expectations upon him throughout his high school career.

During Dan's junior season, he led the team to a 14–0 championship season. The next year, everybody expected nothing less than a repeat. Then

Claremont lost a game, and everybody began to question whether they had what it took, even if they were truly fielding the same team. After that loss, and in the face of fans' criticisms, Dan and the rest of the team played as if they were on a mission. They bowled over opponent after opponent en route to another championship season.

The practice of following high school athletes gained prominence during Dan's playing days. Nowadays, National Signing Day probably gets a lot more attention than it warrants. Kids call press conferences with several colleges' hats in front of them before they dramatically reveal their decisions. The whole circus is a little over the top, but college football fans are crazy about their sport and love tracking their alma mater's recruits for the upcoming season.

By his senior year, many people considered Dan the top high school quarterback prospect in the country. A lot was written about him. His name seemed forever linked to Jeff George, quarterback at Warren Central High School outside of Indianapolis. It was always the two of them, and the debate centered on where they would go and who would fare better in his collegiate career. Mark's name had occasionally appeared in the paper during his high school career, noted as the right-handed hurler who could hit the ball a mile. But it was nothing like this. The local news networks appeared at our school. Everyone wanted to write about Dan.

Of all my brothers, Dan was the one who picked on me the most because we're the closest in age. But we were also very close. Dan drove me to school every morning in his Volkswagen Beetle; it had a souped-up engine and a license plate that read TD POWER. Let me tell you, there was nothing like being in eighth or ninth grade with your older brother not only the star of the school but in the national spotlight.

Unlike Mark, Dan was extremely outgoing and social. His classmates nominated him for homecoming king, he had a girlfriend who went to a different school—a feather in any high school guy's cap—and was extremely popular. He wasn't a huge partier, but he was constantly around friends.

Oftentimes, he'd invite a big group of guys and girls to our house to go swimming—and there I was with my buddy Jack, freshman guys around all those senior girls. Sure, I was out of my league, but I never complained a bit!

Dan became a celebrity in high school, but he never let it go to his head. He never changed, even with all the success that followed. I've always thought it was pretty amazing, considering all the people who were making a fuss over him. How many 18-year-olds can stay grounded with colleges all over the country knocking down his door? The Dan McGwire–Jeff George debate wasn't just of interest in Southern California. People across the country were interested in what schools would sign the top two quarterbacks in America.

Dan shattered plenty of school records during his time at Claremont. He wasn't just tall, he was strong. Tackling him would gas even the strongest defensive linemen. And even when they did manage to get a hold on him, his strength helped him to somehow get the pass off successfully before going down. I don't think anybody will ever come close to breaking Dan's incredible records.

As a senior in high school, he completed 203 of 328 passes (61.9 percent) for 3,172 yards and 33 touchdowns, while punting for a 40-yard average. Overall, he passed for 6,559 yards and 65 touchdowns.

He was honored as a *Parade* magazine All-American, made *Street & Smith's* Top 50, was a *USA Today* All-American honorable mention, California's 1985 Offensive Player of the Year, and he made the Cal-Hi Sports first team all-state squad.

Recruitment offers came predominantly from schools running wide-open offenses that planned to throw the ball 30 to 40 times per game. There were so many colleges pursuing him that it's a blur trying to remember the ones showing the most interest. I do remember Hayden Fry showing up at the house wearing those dark glasses. He offered a pretty compelling case for attending Iowa, pledging to restructure the offense to suit a 6'8" quarterback. Dan could have gone to college on a football or basketball scholarship, but he didn't leverage one against the other. Instead he chose football based on his own desires. He saw himself as a bigger asset on the football field and reasoned that he had a better chance of getting to the NFL than he did to the NBA. Also, he just liked football better.

Despite the fact that he'd pinned his future on football, he continued playing basketball during his senior season at Claremont. He simply dominated the field. A lot of colleges would have gladly had him sign on the dotted line. But Dan finally decided on the University of Iowa and Hawkeyes football. First, Dan liked Coach Fry, who had quite a famous personality. Fry had enjoyed a lot of success at North Texas State before taking over the program at Iowa in 1979. He began making immediate changes—such as adopting a uniform that resembled that of the Pittsburgh Steelers (who were enjoying a successful run at the time) and painting the interior of the visitor's locker room pink. He'd majored in psychology at Baylor and knew that mental institutions and prisons often painted their walls pink because of the color's soothing effects. He wanted opposing teams to be passive. In addition to being colorful, Fry was a winner, and Iowa became a force in the Big Ten after years of being a doormat. Dan liked the fact that Fry committed himself to his new quarterback. Fry had been so glowing in his praise that he sounded like he was going to reinvent the quarterback position with my 6'8" slinging brother at the helm. Fry would say admiringly of Dan that he could throw the ball downhill. Dan gave up basketball to pursue football full time.

After all of the circus regarding where Dan and George would play their college ball, both could have chosen the same school. George had been scheduled to make a visit to Iowa City shortly after Dan signed his letter of intent. But before he got there, Fry called George and asked him to cancel the trip; he no longer had a scholarship for him. George ended up at Purdue University.

A lot of great things started happening for our family all at once. Mark began the 1986 season at Huntsville of the Double-A Southern League, where he hit 10 home runs in 195 at-bats while hitting .303 in 55 games to earn a promotion to Tacoma of the Triple-A Pacific Coast League. At Tacoma, he continued to tattoo the baseball, hitting 13 home runs in 295 at-bats while hitting .318 to earn a call-up to the big leagues on August 22, 1986. I missed his major league debut in Oakland because I had football commitments of my own, but I do remember seeing Mark's first major league home run on satellite television at my friend Jack's house in Claremont. He played in 18 games, 16 of them at third base, and hit .189 with three home runs. He hadn't posted great numbers, but he had made an impression. The A's knew what they had. They saw batting practice when Mark uncoiled to drive the ball over the wall, teammates such as Dave Kingman and a young Jose Canseco looking on and shaking their heads in disbelief at his immense power.

Meanwhile, Dan went to Iowa City to begin his collegiate career as the backup to Mark Vlasic, who had been All-American Chuck Long's backup for three years. Hawkeye fans saw the promise Dan brought to the program early on. In a September 1986 game against the University of Texas at El Paso, Vlasic left the game nursing a sore shoulder, and Dan stepped in to throw touchdown passes of 59 and 54 yards in a 69–7 Iowa victory. Dan was the backup for most of his freshman season, but it was clear that he would be Iowa's quarterback in 1987.

Dan didn't lift weights much, so I spent a lot of time at the Gold's Gym, lifting weights with my buddies. When Dan left for college, I missed having him around, even if we had lived different lives with different friends. Besides, life was good now as the only child left at home. For starters, Dan's Volkswagen became mine. I didn't have to ask permission to use a car or depend on somebody else for a ride; I could come and go as I pleased. Suddenly I was Mr. Independent. I didn't have to share anything with anybody.

Mom and Dad weren't nearly as strict with me as they had been with my brothers, which is probably typical of most parents. It wasn't as if they didn't care; the rules were just a lot more relaxed. I was drinking with my buddies in high school. My parents often traveled during the weekends to watch Mark play, so I had the house to myself a lot—the ticket for an instant party at the McGwire house. When my parents finally found out, I promised them I wouldn't do it anymore—just like I promised I wouldn't go out and shoot BB guns. I didn't care about the rules; I just wanted to have fun.

I was still focused on sports, but I became single-minded about football. I started hitting the weights hardcore so that I could make the varsity football team as a sophomore. I knew I was good enough to play varsity, but at the same time I was struggling to play with one eye. I still had doubts about my limitations, but I never wavered in my determination about going out for and making the varsity team. I worked hard that summer, lifting to prepare for summer football camp. I decided I wanted to make the switch to defense. The coaches decided to put me on the line, where I had to beat out a senior to win the position.

My insecurities went out the window once I put on the pads and began hitting with the seniors. I thought, I *can play with these guys whether I have just one eye or not*; my confidence shot through the roof, and I started to kick some butt.

I made it onto the team, but the senior started the first two games at the position before getting injured. Taking advantage of my opportunity, I had a breakout game with a couple of sacks and a half-dozen tackles. After that, the position was all mine. Before the season was over, I had made second-team All-Baseline League as a sophomore, an accomplishment I credit to weight training. I had become a chiseled 6'3", 205-pound lean, mean athlete. My confidence couldn't have been any greater. I was a one-eyed sophomore varsity letterman—and darn proud of it.

chapter | six

The Rookies

Mark burst onto the national sports scene during his rookie season in 1987. All of a sudden, "Big Mac" seemed to connect for a home run every day. But while Mark's rookie year had been incredible, Dan's went south.

Mark burst onto the national sports scene during his rookie season in 1987. All of a sudden, "Big Mac" seemed to connect for a home run every day. There was even talk of him breaking Roger Maris' single-season home run record. But it didn't happen right away. He began the 1987 season where he'd finished in 1986, making the team as a non-roster invitee, and was off to a slow start on the new season.

Anybody could see Mark's power potential. But the A's didn't seem to know how they wanted to use it. Rob Nelson began the season at first base, Carney Lansford at third, and Reggie Jackson as designated hitter, leaving Mark in limbo as the designated utility player. Mark played games at first, third, DH, and even right field as he struggled to find his way. He hit his first home run in the fourth game of the season on April 10 off of Angels' right-hander Donnie Moore, but he sputtered after that. After 14 games, he still had just one home run under his belt and a limp .136 batting average. Fortunately for Mark, Nelson wasn't performing well either. After Nelson struck out 12 times in his first 24 at-bats, the A's booted him to Triple-A Tacoma. Mark took over the position, but he still struggled at the plate, hitting just five home runs in the A's first 28 games.

Then the dam broke. He hit 14 home runs in the A's next 20 games, including one series in which he dismantled Detroit, hitting five home runs and driving in seven runs in three games. With 19 home runs in the first two months of the season, Mark was within one home run of Mickey Mantle's record 20 home runs in the first two months of the season, which "the Mick" set in 1956. And just like that, the A's had a new first baseman, and the Bay Area had a new hero.

Oakland embraced Mark just as they had Jose Canseco in the previous season, when Canseco won the American League's Rookie of the Year Award after hitting 33 home runs and 117 RBIs. Just like that, Mark was front-page news. Seeing him succeed lit a fire in me, too.

My parents purchased a satellite dish, and we watched most of Mark's games on TV.

Mark continued to dazzle, tying a major league record in Cleveland on June 27 and 28 when he hit five home runs in two games and scored nine. By July 5, he was leading the major league with 30 home runs. He had 33 before the All-Star break, becoming the first rookie in major league history to do so. Heading into the break, Mark had homered in 11 of his previous 16 games. He was on pace with Maris' 1961 season mark. Ironically, Maris hit his 61st home run on October 1, 1961, exactly two years before Mark was born.

Mark wasn't elected a starter on the American League All-Star team that year. But American League manager John McNamara selected him as a reserve for the game, which was played in Oakland that season.

The media grilled Giamatti about the prospect of baseball's sudden rise in home runs, concluding that where there was smoke, there was fire. The intellectual Giamatti, who graduated from Yale and would die of a massive heart attack two years later, was asked if the baseballs were juiced and replied, "Is the ball juiced? No more than I am, sir." Technically speaking, he was right. The balls might not have been juiced, but some of the batters were—and pitchers, too.

I was eager to visit Mark at some point that summer. Football practice would begin in August, so I traveled to Oakland in July. Mark provided me with first-class treatment, as usual. He sent somebody to pick me up at the airport and chauffeur me to the game. I couldn't help thinking about the last time I had attended a major league game at the Coliseum. Mark had been sitting right next to me. Now I was sitting there watching him live his major league dream—and the fans loved him.

Nobody dared go to the restroom or concession stand whenever Mark or Jose Canseco were coming up. They were the kings of Oakland. When Mark's name was announced over the public-address system, the fans went nuts. I would be at the concessions and the fans would run down the corridors, shouting, "McGwire is coming up! McGwire is coming up!" People on the street in the Bay Area stopped me to ask if I was a McGwire (we have quite a family resemblance, all of us). It all made my chest swell with pride.

Mark took me all around the clubhouse during that visit and introduced me to everyone, including Canseco. He was very different from my brother, obviously. For starters, he joked around all the time; he always had something to say about everything. Jose is the kind of guy who liked to dress to the nines, while Mark dressed in jeans and plain button-down shirts. Jose was flamboyant in every way, and Mark was conservative.

At that time, Jose wasn't so yoked up yet. He got a lot bigger later on. In his book *Juiced,* he claims to have starting taking steroids in the minor leagues. That surprised me, given his body in those early A's days. If he was using steroids, then he must not have known how to lift, because he was just lean, with no mass development. If anyone had asked me whether I thought Jose Canseco was using steroids at that time, I would have replied, "Absolutely not." But I was just 17, and I knew nothing about steroids other than the fact that the guys I saw in the muscle magazines used them.

Being inside a clubhouse with professional athletes did not physically intimidate me. Even at 18, I was a lot bigger and more muscular than most of the A's players. I remember hearing comments from the guys on the team that Mark's little brother was kind of yoked. They were impressed with the physique I had at such a young age.

Mark and his wife lived in a nice complex in Alameda, a small island next to Oakland in the San Francisco Bay. He was only earning $62,500 that season—nothing compared to the numbers players make today. In addition to the excitement Mark was creating with his bat during his rookie season, Mark and Kathy were expecting their first child in October. It was a lot of stuff for a guy of 23 years to handle, but he never seemed to worry. Nothing seemed to really affect him one way or the other.

Helping him a lot during that epic rookie season were the many veterans who surrounded him on the A's. Reggie Jackson, who had known Mark since he saw him in a Team USA exhibition game, teased my brother, saying that when he hit home runs they didn't just leave the ballpark, they left the ballpark by a such great distance that he needed to watch them fly out. Mark didn't buy into it then, but later in his career he did start to watch the distances of the ball. And why not—the bombs that Mark hit were moon shots! That's what the fans came to see, home runs that don't land. And no one hit home runs like Mark did.

By the time Mark became Reggie's teammate, Jackson was 41 and a sure lock for the Hall of Fame. He was a sounding board for Mark, as were Ron Cey and Dwayne Murphy. Not only were the A's slugging home runs, they were showing signs of life as a team. In addition to Mark, catcher Terry Steinbach and outfielder Luis Polonia joined the A's that season.

The older guys taught Mark how to handle the media, and he handled reporters with composure, always thanking them afterward. He had manners and knew how to be polite to the press and the fans. When he got a curtain call from the Coliseum crowd during his rookie season for hitting his second home run of a game, Mark reluctantly moved to the top step of the dugout, but not far enough to where most of the fans attending the game could see him. Being humble has always been his way. Later in his career, I remember a heckler unloading on Mark, saying he was going to strike out and hurling other epithets. Mark stepped up to the plate and hit a home run. When he returned to the dugout, he offered a little smile and a wink to the heckler.

On August 11, 1987, Mark connected for his 38th home run of the season to tie the rookie mark for home runs that had been set by Frank Robinson and Wally Berger. Keeping things in proper perspective, Mark celebrated by taking Kathy out for burritos after the game. Three nights later, Mark homered off future Hall of Famer Don Sutton for his 39th home run and a new rookie home-run record—and it was only August 14.

In the midst of Mark's epic rookie season, Dan prepared to lead Iowa as the starting quarterback in his sophomore season. Hayden Fry talked about Dan all the time, touting how my brother's arm was the strongest he'd ever had at Iowa. A story had come out of the Iowa spring game that said Dan threw a ball from his own 25-yard line and hit the face mask of his receiver at the goal line when the receiver lost the ball in the sun. Dan went along with the exaggeration, telling everyone that he hoped to reinvent the position with his height and that the reason he had chosen Iowa was because of their passing attack.

On August 29, Mark hit his 40th home run, a solo shot off Mark Eichhorn in the tenth inning that gave the A's a 6–5 win over the Blue Jays at Toronto. The next night, Dan started against the University of Tennessee in the Kickoff Classic at Giants Stadium. Dan was getting increased attention being Mark McGwire's younger brother. He was consistently mentioned during the telecasts of nationally broadcast baseball games. And at 6'8", a lot of people looked at him as an oddity. It was a lot of scrutiny for a college sophomore carrying a whole program on his shoulders. Everybody was caught up in Mark McGwire, Rookie Home Run Sensation, including the public-address announcer at Giants Stadium who had to correct himself during Dan's introduction when he offered, "At quarterback for Iowa, Mark...*Dan* McGwire."

Iowa lost the game 19–14, the start of a disappointing season for Dan that ended with him being replaced by Chuck Hartlieb.

On September 29, Mark hit a solo home run off Cleveland's John Farrell in the first inning to give him 49 on the season. He went homerless in the next four games, and with one game remaining and the A's out of playoff contention, Mark opted to fly home to be with Kathy during the birth of their son Matthew on October 4.

Mark really showed me something by doing that, rather than chasing 50 homers, which a lot of people wanted him to do. I thought that was really cool. But that's how Mark has always been; he's never looked at records as a big deal. He even told me so. He said, "I will never have another first-born child, but I will have another chance to hit 50." It showed me that his priorities were in order, and it made me look up to him even more.

Once the 1987 season went in the books, Mark turned his attention to 1988. Tony La Russa had just finished his first full season as the A's manager. Mark had liked him from the beginning. He felt really good about the team's chances to become a winner. La Russa brought a different approach to the game and seemed to have the magic touch when it came to resurrecting players' careers. Consider Dennis Eckersley: He had been a starter throughout his entire career, pitching for the Indians, Red Sox, and Cubs before he was traded to the A's prior to the 1987 season. Eckersley still had pinpoint control and quality stuff, he just couldn't take it as deep into the game as he once could. La Russa decided to put him in the bullpen, where he continued to tinker with Eckersley's role until creating what came to be known as "the closer," a guy who would enter the game with his team leading in the final inning and close the door. Eckersley finished the 1987 season with 16 saves and turned into a lethal weapon out of the bullpen. They would be the first 16 saves of a Hall of Fame career that saw him accrue 390.

Dave Stewart was another La Russa project. He came to Oakland in 1986 having spent most of his career in limbo, alternating between starter and reliever, never winning more than 10 games in a season. Under La Russa, Stewart established himself in 1987 as the A's top starter when he went 20–13. By the end of the 1990 season, Stewart had four consecutive 20-win seasons. The A's finished the 1987 season even at 81–81, but Mark could see great things for where the talent would take the team, particularly under a strategist like La Russa.

Given my brothers' success, I felt like the golden child at Claremont High in the fall of 1987. Everyone knew who my brothers were, so coaches and teachers would come up to me and ask how they were doing, showering praise on them. I liked the attention and felt proud of my brothers.

Mark and Kathy lived in Orange County in the off-season, so I saw Mark a lot. I even got to accompany him on a visit to see Reggie Jackson that summer. Reggie had a warehouse full of cars in Newport Beach, and he took us to see his car collection. We talked about all the different cars he had, from Porsches and Ferraris to the classics. Reggie was a terrific host that day, and I left the visit with stars in my eyes.

In November, Mark received an exclamation point on his year when he was named the unanimous choice of the Baseball Writers Association of America as the American League Rookie of the Year, only the second player to win the honor unanimously. (Carlton Fisk received a unanimous vote when he won the award after his rookie season with the Red Sox in 1972.)

While Mark's rookie year had been incredible, Dan's went south. Despite being the best quarterback at Iowa, he didn't get much playing time. He finished the season with 47 of 84 completed passes, for 680 yards, six touchdowns, and four interceptions. There was a lot written about what went wrong—one of the Iowa coaches called him "impatient," but I don't think that was the problem. In my opinion, it boiled down to a personality conflict between Dan and Bill Snyder, Fry's offensive coordinator. Snyder had coached with Fry at North Texas State and moved to Iowa with him in 1979. Snyder later went on to be head coach at Kansas State, where he had great success before retiring (and unretiring to again coach at KSU).

Dan is an easygoing guy. I have a feeling that Snyder's straight-laced approach might have caused some static for them. Whatever the problem was, Dan felt that he was benched unfairly, leading him to look into playing somewhere else.

chapter | seven

The Splash

While Mark picked up his first championship ring, Dan was busy picking up where he left off, taking over quarterbacking duties at San Diego State. I wasn't motivated about anything besides lifting weights and partying. But I was 18 and on top of the world, so what did I care?

After Mark's auspicious rookie season, the limelight followed. Suddenly, people recognized him wherever he went. Fans approached him in restaurants and interrupted him for autographs, no matter what he was doing. All he wanted to do was do his job, play well, and go home at the end of the day. Mark never relished the attention that went along with his talent, and he began to crave privacy.

In addition to the increased attention, Mark also found that expectations were raised for his performance in the coming season. After all, if he could hit 49 home runs as a rookie, why wouldn't he break Roger Maris' record the next year? I felt for Mark. All he really wanted to be was a baseball player and stay true to himself. He didn't want or need all the external trimmings of fame—the glamour of it all. But he was famous whether he liked it or not. On the bright side, Mark signed a new contract with the A's for $260,000 in 1988.

Meanwhile, Dan hoped to carve out a new beginning for himself at San Diego State.

Once Dan made it clear that he wanted to leave Iowa, San Diego State made overtures to have him join their ranks. As is typical for a transfer athlete, Dan had to sit out a year before he could play out his final two seasons of eligibility. San Diego State coach Al Luginbill planned to build his offense around Dan after his redshirt season.

Dan seemed really happy with the change—we all were, since everyone felt that he got a raw deal at Iowa. Despite being redshirted, his new teammates saw Dan's immense skills, and he gained a lot of respect for his work ethic in practice.

My junior year at Claremont was going well. I continued to pursue weight lifting and football. And with Dan now closer to home, I visited him on weekends to live it up. He shared an apartment with some of the guys on the football team, and they had a ball. San Diego State had a reputation for being a party school, and it was well deserved. Every guy there was on a steady diet of chicks and beer.

I brought some friends along on one visit, and Dan and some of his teammates took us to Tijuana, Mexico. Let's just say I had a *great* time. The clubs were jam-packed, and there were girls everywhere. I'm sure my brother and his friends got a rise out of taking me and my friends to a place like that, but trust me, we weren't complaining.

I got away with a lot for a high school kid, but I never did anything too crazy. If my parents asked me to be home by midnight, I was home by midnight. I got decent grades. I worked hard in sports. After school, I lifted weights. They knew that I wasn't out looking for trouble.

My parents had sued the insurance company of the parents of the kid who gave me the BB gun, which resulted in a settlement of $150,000. The money went into a trust fund I was able to receive once I turned 18, which I did at the end of my junior year at Claremont High. I blew a chunk of that money right away on a 1988 black I-ROC Z Camaro convertible. I had a job at my Dad's office that gave me all the income I needed, about $300 a month, cleaning the dental office in the building he built.

My parents spent a good amount of that summer in Oakland, and I spent it partying. I just hung out, partied with friends, pumped iron, and went to football practice. I visited Mark a couple of times that summer, but I was also interested in my own stuff. I played on a football passing league and spent a lot of time at the beach and Parker Strip, Arizona, a spot on the banks of the Colorado River.

The A's got off to an incredible start in 1988 and quickly became the envy of baseball due to a combination of things: Sandy Alderson's innovative and shrewd moves as the general manager, Tony La Russa's intelligent managing, and the team's wealth of young talent.

Alderson knew he had a nice collection of young players with Mark, Jose Canseco, Terry Steinbach, and Walt Weiss, and he felt that the best way to augment that talent would be to bring in a group of professionals who were motivated and liked to win. Among the players he brought in were Don Baylor, Glenn Hubbard, Dave Henderson, and Dave Parker. It worked. The

A's went from 81 wins in 1987 to 104 in 1988, winning the American League West division.

Mark didn't quite reach the heights of his rookie season, but that was partly because opposing pitchers began using a different approach against him. It was one to which Mark eventually took exception. In a game against the Angels in May, Mark hit a home run off of Kirk McCaskill. In Mark's next at-bat, the pitcher beaned him in the head. His helmet prevented a serious injury, but Mark was pissed. He wanted to charge the mound but restrained himself. After the game, he told the media that the next time somebody buzzed the light tower, they were going to have to deal with him charging the mound.

Mark hit .260 for the season with 32 home runs and 99 RBIs. Still, he had a presence. Texas right-hander Kevin Brown said of Mark, "Any time a guy that big steps up to the plate—they're very few and far between, thank God—it's kind of hard not to notice him standing there. The sun just disappears for a while."

The 1988 season belonged to Canseco, who became the first player to do the 40–40 thing by hitting 42 home runs and steal 40 bases. He also had 124 RBIs and was named the American League's Most Valuable Player.

Mark and Jose's home run totals were pretty amazing considering where they played. Oakland Coliseum was legendary in baseball as a place where home runs went to die. It was certainly not a hitter's ballpark. I honestly believe Mark or Jose would have broken Maris' record during their earlier years had they not played in Oakland. That park may have robbed both of them of 20 home runs.

"The Bash Brothers," as Mark and Canseco came to be known, had taken the town by storm. While they respected each other as teammates, they were not close. It was inevitable, given their age and talents, that a natural rivalry was born, complete with jealousy on both sides. I suspect that this rivalry is what gave way to some of the more outlandish claims in Canseco's memoir, *Juiced*. Mark is a private person who has a small circle of people whom he trusts. I find it absurd that Canseco would be inside that circle. It just doesn't make sense to me. It never has. It's well known that Canseco has courted press by saying grandiose things. Just read his books. "The Bash Brothers" was a label created by the Athletics, and Mark and Canseco were strong teammates. A brotherhood it was not.

In the 1988 playoffs, the A's easily handled the Red Sox in the American League Championship Series. Everybody expected them to steamroll the Dodgers in the World Series. The press depicted the matchup as a David vs. Goliath, the Dodgers the upstart David that had upset the New York Mets to advance. The Athletics were a complete team, balanced with power and great pitching. The Dodgers, many said, had ridden the coattails of Orel Hershiser all season. Their right-hander had won 23 games and set a major league record during the regular season by throwing 59 consecutive score-less innings before gaining a win and a save in the National League Championship Series against the Mets.

Dodger Stadium hosted the first two games of the World Series, and Mark got us tickets. Dan brought one of his friends, and I brought one of mine for that game. What a thrill to see Mark out there playing in the World Series! It was incredible. And that first game was a rout by the A's.

Jose Canseco flexed his muscles in the second inning when he hit a bullet toward center field off Tim Belcher for a grand slam to give the A's a 4–2 lead. We were thrilled. Figuring we'd be stuck in traffic for the rest of our lives if we didn't leave early, we left, confident that the A's were well on their way to a win. We were in the car listening to the game on the radio when Dennis Eckersley gave up one of the most famous home runs in World Series history to Kirk Gibson, whose leg was so banged up he could barely run the bases. We couldn't believe anybody could do that to Eck. He was as close to a sure thing as anybody in baseball at that time.

That game entered the record books as the first time a World Series game had been won by a last-inning, come-from-behind home run win. We were incredibly bummed, so we decided to visit Mark at his hotel and cheer him up. He was with other guys from the team, and they all appeared to be fine. That's one thing you never realize until you're around baseball every day—that you have to let it go. They play so many games that they simply have to leave them behind them. I was stunned. They had just lost the first game of the World Series in a highly unexpected fashion, and yet they treated it as business as usual.

Hershiser started Game 2 and pitched a three-hit shutout and hit 3–3 in a 6–0 Dodgers win to put Los Angeles up 2–0 in the best-of-seven series. Mark had gone hitless in the first two games and had no hits in three at-bats in Game 3 when he stepped to the plate to face Jay Howell with one out in the ninth and the game tied 1–1. I had some friends over to the house, and we were watching when Mark connected for the game-winning homer. While Mark rounded the bases, we went nuts, jumping up and down, pumping our fists. To see my brother win a World Series game with one swing of the bat gave me goose bumps.

Despite Mark's heroics in that third game, the Dodgers took the next two games and the World Series championship. David had stomped Goliath. It was a huge disappointment for Mark and the A's, who had high hopes for a Series win.

Mark's marriage was also suffering. In 1989, he and Kathy divorced. We were all saddened by the news, but it seems to me that they just married too soon; 21 was just simply too young, and he was rarely home.

My senior season of football at Claremont in 1988 was a success. My buddy Aaron Pruitt played linebacker, and I played on the defensive line; together we were the team's big hitters and the strongest guys on the team. We had our moment by reaching the semifinals of the C.I.F. playoffs. And just like that, football season was over. But in my mind, I was already thinking about college ball. Several schools had expressed interest, so I figured I'd play at the next level.

As I headed toward the home stretch of my senior year, I partied like there was no tomorrow. If my parents weren't home, I invited my friends over; if they were home, I found a party elsewhere. I'd invite my close guy friends over and we'd hang out all day drinking, swimming, and barbecuing. Then we'd call some girls to come over and hang out until the noise got too loud and one of the neighbors called the police. They'd shut down the party outside, so we'd just take it indoors. The pool was our beer cooler, and we put soap in the Jacuzzi to suds it up. We drank out of beer bongs and played quarters.

Sometimes we'd go out looking for fights, and other times they'd find us. We were the biggest guys around and we didn't take lip service from anybody. The friends I partied with and trained with could all bench more than 400 pounds by the end of our senior year. Some of my friends loved to fight. Most times I didn't get involved, but I just stood there to make sure that nobody cold cocked one of my friends. My buddies and I never lost a fight. We were animals because a bunch of us were juicing and drinking, not to mention we were teenagers. A word to the wise: Don't ever get in a fight with someone taking steroids and drinking alcohol—they are two powerful drugs that make an intense combination.

Suffice it to say, I wasn't motivated about anything at the time besides lifting weights and partying. But I was 18 and on top of the world, so what did I care? With the settlement, I felt like I had a bottomless pit of money. I had it all. What could possibly go wrong?

* * *

Mark suffered the first in a series of injuries in April of the 1989 season, with a herniated disc. Jose Canseco was out with a wrist fracture. In addition to Canseco's injury, he had other troubles off the field. When he went to get his wrist X-rayed, someone spotted a semiautomatic pistol on the floor of his Jaguar, prompting an arrest of the reigning American League MVP. Even so, without their two best sluggers, the A's kept rolling in 1989.

Mark returned to play after 14 games and reached a milestone on July 5, 1989, when he hit a three-run homer off Kansas City's Charlie Leibrandt to give him 100 career home runs. The home run came in Mark's 1,400th at-bat; only one player, Ralph Kiner, had reached 100 home runs sooner.

The A's were still a well-rounded team. They had a quality defense; a stellar roster of pitchers, including Bob Welch, Dave Stewart, Mike Moore, and Storm Davis; and they reacquired Rickey Henderson, which helped the offense score even when they weren't hitting home runs. They made it back to the World Series, this time against their rivals from across the Bay, the San Francisco Giants.

The A's won the first two games in Oakland, and then the series headed across the Bay to San Francisco. When the earthquake hit San Francisco, I panicked. I was watching the game on TV and didn't know what was going on. My parents and my brother were there. I was a wreck. At the time, I was a self-absorbed teenager, and I didn't think much about anything or anyone else. But that earthquake affected me. Fortunately, Candlestick Park remained intact, and no one was injured. My parents were stuck in traffic and hadn't yet made it to the stadium. But 67 died that day, and the damage could be seen everywhere. In the wake of the disaster, Major League Baseball postponed the Series. Some felt it should be cancelled altogether. But on October 27, after an 11-day delay, the World Series resumed.

The A's took the final two games to complete the sweep. Mark didn't hit a home run during the Series, but he hit .343 during the postseason, which helped erase his frustrations from the previous year. People started talking about a dynasty. And why shouldn't they? Mark and Jose were young, franchise players—not a bad foundation for a team to have.

While Mark picked up his first championship ring, Dan was busy picking up where he left off. He didn't miss a beat taking over as the quarterback at San Diego State. Al Luginbill instituted a wide-open passing offense with four receivers and one back that took full advantage of Dan's abilities. It fit him like a glove. They played out of a shotgun formation so he could get momentum moving downfield; it made him feel like he could whip a pass anywhere. His go-to play was to throw from one hash mark across the field to a receiver near the far sideline. It was one of the more difficult passes in any quarterback's repertoire, but he had the line of vision and the arm strength to pull off the dangerous pass, throwing over the defense. He was a great leader, and his team was behind him 100 percent. The results came immediately. By the end of his first season at San Diego State, he had thrown for 3,651 yards, and the NFL scouts were circling, drooling just thinking about the revolutionary possibilities of having a quarterback of Dan's size.

chapter | eight

The Weight

It started innocently: Take your vitamins, eat right, and use the right supplements. Over time, I began to establish relationships with some of these guys. I wanted to gain entrance into the community of bodybuilders; I wanted to belong.

Senioritis affects a lot of high school seniors the same way, but they didn't have money in the bank; I did. Weight training totally captured me in high school. It had at first been a means to an end, a method to help me overcome being blind in one eye and become a better football player. After a while, it became an obsession.

During my sophomore year I signed up for my first gym membership at Gold's Gym in Upland. Once a member, I lived at the place and knew I belonged. Everybody has a place where he feels most comfortable; for me that was it. As my weight training continued, I moved to the Deer Creek Athletic Club in Rancho Cucamonga in 1987 and then the World Gym in Pomona in 1988. It was at the World Gym that my program really took off.

By my junior year in high school, I had already gained plenty of strength, muscle, and size. I was 220 pounds and I could bench 335 and squat 350. Around the gym, people talked about steroids. The World Gym and Gold's Gym were big havens for bodybuilders, and steroids were just another part of the program for them. People weren't freaked out about using steroids back then; discussion about them was all out in the open.

My knowledge about weight lifting had increased exponentially since my brother and I first picked up those concrete-filled weights in our garage. Over the years, a handful of bodybuilders had me under their wing and showed me different techniques and movements, teaching me how to train smart and not to overdo it. It started innocently: Take your vitamins, eat right, and use the right supplements. Over time, I began to establish relationships with some of these guys. I wanted to gain entrance into the community of bodybuilders; I wanted to belong.

The World Gym had mostly free weights, dumbbells, barbells, cables, and a handful of seated movements. It had positioned itself as a gym for hardcore weight-training guys. It wasn't a health club. There were no women bouncing to aerobic routines, no wimps running nautilus machines. This was the real deal.

My buddies and I who worked out there were substantially younger than the rest of the clientele. Most of the guys were bodybuilders, many of them competitive, and power lifters. These were guys who hung out at the gym all day long and were 10, 15 years older than us. We were in awe. Eventually, we started talking to the guys, asking them how to get big, if we were doing the movements right…that sort of thing. I thought I knew a lot until I started picking their brains.

Eventually steroids came up in conversation. Some of them sold steroids themselves, but those who didn't knew guys who did. They all worked out hard and they all boosted with steroids. I felt like an apprentice learning from the master of a trade. I felt they recognized how serious I was about becoming an accomplished bodybuilder.

It was in this atmosphere, where I felt most comfortable and at home, that I decided I wanted to try steroids. I didn't know about the downside. All I saw were the results—and I was surrounded by them. I considered steroids just another element of my workout, something that was going to enhance my strength and size. Even though so much more is known about steroids, I think that's how kids approach them today. As a kid, you're invincible. And any quick avenue to gain muscle and size is a good one. Believe me, I understand the seduction—the bottom line is, you got results. You got discernibly bigger and stronger. Despite all the gains I had made at the gym naturally, I saw steroids as the magic elixir that would take me to the next step. For me, taking them was so easy to justify.

Early in 1989, the last semester of my senior year at Claremont, I began asking some of the more seasoned lifters in the gym about steroids. None of them were out recruiting young bodybuilders to become steroid users, but I knew who to seek out. Some of my buddies who worked out with me were interested as well. We'd been around the gym, we knew who was and who wasn't using, and the differences were compelling. The older guys in the gym could tell we were serious lifters, and I think we earned our way into this body building alliance with our desire and accomplishment. We were ready.

After a lot of discussion and debate, my buddies and I decided we didn't want to get stuck with a needle, so injections were off the table. We asked if we could get something in a pill form. The guy who helped us out suggested we begin with a steroid called Anavar, a substance that burns fat and adds strength. It's probably one of the mildest oral steroids out there, not much for helping you bulk up or gain a lot of weight. It is fairly mild on the body and not very toxic—I think that's probably why he recommended it to us youngsters. He knew it would help us gain strength but that it wouldn't hurt us. In fact, because it has a relative lack of side effects, Anavar is frequently the steroid of choice for many top-level female bodybuilders and other athletes.

I started my daily dosage at 50 milligrams before topping out at 100 milligrams. The results were good. I also felt vibrant and always full of energy. I improved my bench press to 405 pounds from 375, my squats to 425 from 375, and my dead lift to 445 from 385 as a senior. I also added 10 pounds of muscle to my frame in just three months.

I got off on seeing my body growing right before my eyes. Before using steroids, I worked out around 90 minutes, five days a week. Once I began taking Anavar, my workouts swelled to two hours or more. Steroids didn't lift the weights for me, but they sure gave me the capacity to lift more.

Even though I had made tremendous gains by myself through training hard and eating well, I couldn't believe the results I had achieved in such a short amount of time. Of course, I can't attribute all of my gains at the time to Anavar. At 18 and 19, I had great genetics working for me, too. Unfortunately, I didn't see that back then. All I saw was a shortcut. I thought about what I might achieve in my future. The sky was the limit.

My entire life, I had wanted to be an athlete, picturing myself as a basketball, baseball, or football player of the highest order. Football had earned me scholarship offers to San Diego State, where I could have joined Dan, or Oregon State. I visited both campuses and liked them both. I also liked the idea of playing college football. And yet, going to college didn't appeal to me. I had been a slow learner my entire life, but I managed to eke out average grades in high school. I graduated with a 2.85 grade point average—nothing to brag about, yet nothing for me to hang my head in shame about either. I just felt like school wasn't for me—even if it meant playing college football. Besides, I had a nice nest egg in the bank in my settlement, even though I had begun chipping away at it more regularly. That money was all mine—my parents didn't know what I was spending it on. I was buying steroids and living what seemed to be an ongoing party. I liked to take friends out to dinner and spend extravagantly. At the time, $150,000 was a lot of money. To me, a teenager, it seemed limitless.

I felt like I was living the high life. Why would I screw it all up by going to college? My parents wanted me to go. They warned me about spending all of my money. But who were they to tell me anything? I knew better than they did. I'd made up my mind; I wasn't going to attend college, and my parents weren't about to change my mind.

Once I graduated from high school, my life was all partying and pumping steel. I was still living at home, and being a total slug did not play well there. Naturally, my parents were concerned about what I would do with my life. I'd already opted to forego college, and now I wasn't doing anything at all. So I moved from home to my own place. First to an apartment in Upland with a friend and then to Pomona with two friends. Our place was a real party palace, with a concrete backyard that became the site for countless keggers. I had partied throughout high school and just kept it going after high school, hanging out with the girls, drinking, and trying to find myself. I didn't know who I was at that time. I was lost; I was searching for something.

That summer of 1989, I added 50 to 100 milligrams a day of Dianabol (Dbol), a fast-acting oral. I had joined a new gym in Upland, where I made another connection for steroids, this time the hardcore stuff. The jump from Anavar to Dbol was dramatic; Dbol had much higher testosterone levels.

Equipoise, Primobolan, and Deca Durabolin were next.

Equipoise is a very powerful drug. I'd buy a cycle of at least 12 weeks, depending on the number of shots per cycle. Injectable steroids are sold by the bottle, so you're buying by the cc (cubic centimeter). Typically, I'd take a shot or two a week for eight to 12 weeks and then get off and let my body clean up. We were taught to cycle on and off. Taking steroids continuously caused too many side effects. Twelve weeks was long enough, then take three to six months off and come back again. That way your body is prepared for you to use again.

Steroids last in your body six to 12 months, depending on the drug. And boy, do you feel a difference. This is where it gets to your psyche—you feel so powerful and almighty, almost invincible when you're on them. When you're off, you feel weak and lethargic. I lost about 10 or 15 percent of my gains on an off-cycle.

Obviously, the step up to Equipoise, Primobolan, and Deca Durabolin brought the needle along with them. Most people wonder what it's like to inject yourself, and I'm here to tell you, it isn't an easy thing to master. I never liked needles; when I was younger, my mom and the nurse had to hold me down at the doctor's office whenever I had to get a shot. But once you're on steroids, you have to do it. My supplier showed me how to inject myself. He did it for me. And if he didn't do the injecting, I had buddies who would, and I'd shoot them. I just didn't have enough nerve to do it myself initially. Eventually I got over my fear of the needle. I didn't like having to depend on somebody else to inject me. Plus, it was worth it. I learned how to shoot up in my shoulder and hip, two areas with a lot of muscle. Once I got it right, I didn't even feel the sting of the needle. I got good at it.

It's a real rush, taking a shot and knowing that within a matter of days and weeks you're going to get huge. It's a high that makes you want to work out harder and do everything more aggressively, because you know that stuff is in your system. It takes you over.

Pills were kid stuff compared to these injectable steroids. And besides, taking pills is harder on the liver. Using the needle is safer for long-term use. Taking a pill like Anavar felt more like an amino acid pill; even though I got results, they came at a markedly slower pace. The high-testosterone injectables came rock-hard with powerfully greater results. It was an aggressive way to do steroids, not only in its results but in the way it affected my mood. I got a high just knowing it was the real deal. I was going to get huge like the Hulk. I was going to dominate. I felt a substantial difference right away both physically and psychologically.

I got a particular rush from injecting any steroids that were oil based. First off, I had to really press hard on the needle to inject it, because the stuff is like syrup or motor oil. It takes some force to get it through the syringe and into your body. After injection, I had to massage the site in order to prevent scar tissue. I'd always be a little sore in the hip area the next day, as if I could still feel that shot. To me that meant that the stuff really was working. I looked forward to the next time I was due for a shot. My body tingled in anticipation for that syrupy sweet elixir.

It was during this period that my knowledge of steroids, nutrition, and everything else that related to bodybuilding grew exponentially. I had finally found something that I was enthusiastic to learn about, and I became a sponge. My teachers were bodybuilders and power lifters. Bodybuilders know more about steroids, nutrition, and building muscle than anybody. Steroids were a fairly common practice, and an advanced bodybuilder was more educated on the topic than any football player, baseball player, or other athlete. The sport practically required it in order to build strength and size. The results that steroids provided bodybuilders didn't enhance their performance—the results *were* their performance.

The more I advanced using steroids, the more I began to mix, or stack, what I was using. The ideal way to use steroids and build muscle is to not use a number of different kinds at once. I did what other bodybuilders did and experimented to see which ones worked best. There are plenty to choose from. Everyone's body chemistry is different, and there's a great variation in the results people get from different steroids. I tried to figure out which ones worked best for me. It was a process of elimination that took some time, since results wouldn't come for a while after injection.

Most Equipoise users notice an increased appetite, and that was true for me, too. That side effect made it impossible for me to diet while using it. A lot of bodybuilders will include Equipoise in a mass cycle when they stack with other agents. Stacking a slow-acting steroid like Equipoise with a fast-acting steroid like D-bol or Anadrol 50 produces immediate effects. The end result is that you start seeing results within the first couple weeks of your cycle and continue up until the end of the cycle with long-acting injectables, like Deca or Equipoise, with some kind of testosterone. That way, you reap benefits at the beginning and all the way to the end of the cycle.

Other drugs I used during that period included Anadrol 50, Testosterone Suspension, and Dianabol. Anadrol 50 is a fast-acting oral that allowed me to gain large amounts of weight and strength, but mostly strength, in a relatively short time span. It is heavily toxic, so it is unsuited to long-term use. Taken longer than six to eight weeks, it produces serious side effects and the potential for permanent liver damage. I liked the results, so I'd typically use 50 to 100 milligrams a day for six to eight weeks and then cycle off to something else.

Testosterone Suspension is a water-based injectable, one of the most powerful of the testosterones. An effective dose ranged from 350 to 1,000 milligrams per week, or 50 to 140 milligrams a day. It does not stay in the body for long, which is why the weekly dosage is so high.

A year later, I began to dabble with combinations like Equipoise and Anadrol 50, Dbol, Sten, Halotestin, Sustanon 250, Testoviron, and Testosterone Suspension. I rotated them in different variations. For example, I'd try a combination of Equipoise with Sten or Testoviron for 12 weeks and Anadrol 50 for six to eight weeks. I got really strong on that cycle and watched, in what seemed like an out-of-body experience, as my bench press swelled to 475 pounds. *Who is that guy pushing up all of that weight?* I'd think to myself in amazement. After that, I would try Halotestin or Sten and Dbol. I also used Sustanon 250 or Testosterone Suspension with Deca and Anadrol 50, rotating them to see what combination worked the best; these cycles were for strength and mass only. I also took Nolvadex—used as a first-line defense against breast cancer—to prevent tumor growth in the nipple area, an unfortunate side effect of steroid use. It's a common agent for the prevention of gynocomastia, or "guyno" as it's referred to in the bodybuilding community, but its long-term effects were insignificant.

A lot of the mixing and matching was dictated to me by my circumstances. These steroids were black-market drugs, so I couldn't always get my hands on whatever I wanted. I found myself at the mercy of my supplier on many occasions and that meant I had to take what he could get. Money was not an object since I still had a lot of my settlement cash.

When I had steroids pumping through my body, I had huge amounts of energy. It's not that spring-out-of-bed-in-the-morning energy. But lifting weights, the aggression just builds and builds, and you end up getting this ultimate pump. Breaking down muscle tissue supplies more blood flow to the muscle. If you're working your tricep muscles, you're going to feel a lactic-acid (which is what provides "the burn") buildup that causes blood flow to that area. Your heart sends more blood there to begin the healing process and make that burn go away. Lactic acid is the human body's byproduct when muscle is pushed to its limit; the harder you push, the more intense the burn. This is the body's defense from overstress. Without it, people would pull and tear muscles all the time. The body tells you to stop, and most people do because it's incredibly painful. But I loved that burn, and I went after it.

I was headed to a place beyond that burn called a failure set, a place where there is nothing left. And I could get huge, tremendous pumps with the drugs and pretty good pumps when I was off the drugs. Being on steroids just feels good. It does something to you. Your body is doing something that feels incredible, superhuman. It's an awesome high. It's not like other drugs. It's an emotional, mental, and physical high that you create for yourself by pushing your body to the outer limits.

Eventually the pump I got from a workout tapered off. But on a cycle of steroids, that pump lingered a good two to three hours later. I'd be home hours later and still feel it. My clothes fit me tightly, like a superhero. I felt indestructible. I was the Hulk. It's this feeling of indestructibility that got me addicted. I was hooked on the emotion, the idea of being all-powerful. It felt incredible. Steroids became the focal point of my life. I never thought about it as "abuse." I didn't care about the possible side effects or what could happen to me later. I felt like I was in control, like I could stop whenever I wanted to. And why wouldn't I think about the positives, when all the benefits of the drugs were right in front of me, in plain sight? I was focused on becoming the biggest, strongest guy out there—simple as that.

Strength builds muscle. That's how the human body works. Without strength, there is no muscle. The stronger you get, the more durable, but also dense—the muscles get harder and bigger. Muscle tissue gets thicker and thicker with time. Steroids help goose that time frame from years to months. With steroids, you just get there quicker, I reasoned. Simple as that.

Everybody wants to be good at something. This was my something. I didn't need perfect vision to do it. More important, I understood what it took to make gains—hard work and determination. I liked the work and I liked the pain. I considered pain to be the process of weakness leaving the body. I progressed faster than most people around me. At my high school graduation I was 6'3" and a lean 245. My grit in the gym captured people's attention. And everyone knew the McGwire name at that time—my brothers were famous. Dan was a college football star and Mark was in the major leagues. Bodybuilding and strength was Jay's thing, something I had all for my own. I felt I had found my identity. Everybody seemed to love me. I got respect. I was constantly honored and praised for my size and strength. This is Jay, the baby brother of the McGwires, Little Mac! I had no idea where it was going to lead me, I just knew I felt satisfaction. That passion and lifestyle became my life; it became my god.

chapter | nine

The Struggle

In the gym, my friends and I laughed at Mark's routine, but he would just shake his head. He didn't want to lose his swing, he protested. Without fail, he'd say that he didn't want to build bulk and muscle as a baseball player.

In the back of my mind, I suppose I knew I was on a road to nowhere. Partying, lifting weights, and steroid use were about the extent of my existence—somewhere deep down I had to know this was unsustainable. Didn't I?

I'd done well to hold on to my money in high school, but soon I began chipping away fairly significantly at my nest egg, money that should have served me for a long time.

Steroids consumed a fair amount of the money, but I also found myself doing things like picking up dinner checks or buying all the supplies to keeping a never-ending party raging. I was Good Time Jay, and I liked being the object of attention. I knew I was foolish at the time, I just didn't know how to change. I know my parents were worried—my poor choices were obvious to anyone who paid attention—but all they could do was chime in with advice about saving money, buying a house, and investing that nest egg of mine. I had other ideas.

I suspected they were talking to Mark about me, asking him for help to get me back on the right track. Mark always seemed concerned about me, asking questions and offering suggestions. He offered his help, and in 1990 he asked me to move to the Bay Area to work for and live with the Bonadonas, a family that owned a carpet-cleaning business. After Kathy and Mark split, he needed to find someone who could take care of his son Matthew when he was at the ballpark. Mark couldn't do it himself. A friend hooked him up with the Bonadona family. The Bonadonas became Matthew's babysitter when Mark was at the ballpark, and since Mark and the Bonadonas both lived in Alameda, the situation was ideal. After a fashion, Mark became close friends with the family.

In Mark's mind, I suppose he figured that if they could babysit his son, why not his kid brother? The Bonadonas had a close-knit family and they got along with everybody. They had a good carpet cleaning business. Mark pitched them about me, telling them that I was 19 and really didn't know what I wanted to do, that maybe I could work for their business.

Given the freedom I had at my party house with my friends, it was crazy to move to another city to work for and live with a family I didn't even know. But having Mark show an interest in me carried a lot of weight. Plus, if I was honest with myself, I was burned out on partying. I had nothing going except for my body and the steroids. I didn't have a job, and I didn't want to burn through all of my money. I reasoned that a move would be good. Not only would I be able to get away from my friends and make a new start, I would also be able to get closer to my brother, whom I adored.

The experiment worked. The family took me in and made me feel as if I was one of them. Phil and Rose Bonadona—I called them my second mom and dad—loved me, and I loved them right back. They took good care of me.

When I moved, I took a break from steroids, but I still lifted weights seriously. I helped the Bonadona family clean carpets and went to all of the ballgames. I saw Mark all the time, which made the transition easier. I still partied, drank a lot, and had a good time, but I no longer felt like my life was spinning out of control.

I lived in the main house with Phil and Rose; behind that was a guest house, where their daughter Denise lived with her husband Paul and their kids, Megan and Roman. Phil and Rose also had three sons, Morris, Philip Jr., and Joe. Paul, who was a power lifter back in the day, worked out with me at a hole-in-the-wall gym called Iron Island. He loved doing the power movements like squats, dead lifts, and bench presses. That gym was filled with hardcore power lifters, and they had dumbbells up to two hundred pounds, an insane amount of weight for a dumbbell and a rare fixture in the gyms I was used to.

The Bonadonas reminded me of my parents in a lot of ways. They were outgoing, and everyone loved them. My parents and the Bonadonas became great friends and remain close today.

Eating meals with the family proved to be an exquisite dining pleasure. The family is Italian, and Paul grew up in Louisiana. Between Rose's Italian cooking and Paul's Cajun specialties, the meals were unbelievable. And of course, they'd stuff us to the gills. They both loved to cook and made us red beans and rice, white beans and rice, jambalaya…all the Cajun foods. Then there were the sauces, the meatballs, and the sausages…. Everyone cooked. Paulie made incredible cornbread. Everyone had a specialty. I had it made back then. Of course, I gained a lot of unnecessary weight during those years as a result. I also missed workouts occasionally because I worked late, went to the ballgames, and had a few-too-many beers at the ballpark watching Mark.

Inside the Bonadona home, we talked about anything and everything. I talked to Phil like I would any friend—they were all that way. We'd talk about sports, steroids, girls, drinking, partying, and my future. They thought that I would regret it if I didn't give football another try and encouraged me to go after it. But they supported me no matter what I did.

Phil had been a cop for 25 years, so he had plenty of great tales and was an accomplished storyteller. Phil always believed in reaching for your dreams, and he knew how much I wanted to be a professional bodybuilder. But he was also cautious. He knew I had been on steroids, and he wanted me to be careful.

Phil Jr. owned and operated the carpet cleaning business, and he took me to my first Christian church. It was completely different from the Catholic church I experienced during my childhood. After singing praise music and offering prayer, the pastor asked everyone to open their Bibles. I learned more in that one hour at that church than I had in years as a Catholic.

The pastor chose a certain subject for his sermon and selected 15 different verses throughout the old and new testaments to make his point. I felt moved and inspired to go to church more often, but I fought internally with my old nature, which included partying and women. I wasn't ready to embrace church yet, but going to church with Phil Jr. had definitely planted another seed in my heart. I would ultimately see it grow later in my life.

Not only did I love living with the Bonadonas, I also liked the work. I hadn't shown a lot of ambition in Claremont, but I never shied away from hard work. I learned a lot of it from watching my dad growing up, but I also applied the lessons of my bodybuilding. When I still lived at home, all the chores in the house became mine because I had been the last son to leave home. I worked from time to time in construction with my brother Bob. He'd say to me, "You want to work? I'll put you to work," and he'd put me under a house digging the piping trenches for the plumbing. Back in those days, I was earning a dozen donuts for breakfast and whatever was on the menu for lunch—it was enough payment to satisfy me since I'd spend that much in food otherwise.

The Bonadonas' carpet-cleaning business involved a process called chem-dry. You applied a solution to the carpet and then rubbed a pad with a buffer across the carpet's surface. We did residential and commercial jobs. Most commercial work was done after regular working hours, so we had different schedules. We were very busy and worked hard. Normally we'd do four or five houses a day, and we were only one truck; they operated three. Depending on the workload for the day, we worked alone or in pairs.

One great benefit was the hours. A lot of the business we did was in the early morning. If the A's had an afternoon game, say, on a Thursday, we'd be able to go to the game and start the party early.

Mark always left me tickets in the players' parking lot behind the Coliseum. I had a parking pass, so I just drove up, and they waved me through security. After a while I got to know everyone pretty well.

Everybody should have the opportunity to attend sporting events like I did back in the day. No crowds and no waiting in line. It was easy to get spoiled with that kind of preferential treatment. The family section was behind third base, but a lot of times Mark would arrange for us to sit at field level right behind first base. I still got a kick out of hanging out in the clubhouse with those guys; Dave Parker, Dave Henderson, Walt Weiss, and Mike Gallego were all fun guys.

Mark lifted some back then, but he really wasn't a serious weight lifter. He began while at USC, but his workouts weren't serious like mine were. To me, it seemed like he was going through the motions. The program he was doing wasn't going to make him bigger or stronger. And he wasn't too diligent, either.

He trained on and off through the years, but he never established anything consistent. For example, the only exercises he did with his legs were leg extensions, which worked the quads, and leg curls for his hamstrings. He didn't do squats, but he would do some leg presses, which really work the legs. For his upper body, he only did the machines and cables, along with a little dumbbell and barbell work— that's it. Serious lifters didn't train that way. Free weights were the best form of resistance training back then, and they still are. You need strength and balance to develop the proper form to lift free weights.

When we talked about weight training, I always told him that he needed to do more basic power movements if he really wanted to make any gains. Without fail, he'd say that he didn't want to build bulk and muscle as a baseball player. I argued that the secret of resistance training was that the different power movements with great form would isolate each muscle belly that make the muscle grow. Mark wasn't interested, so I didn't push it. And he didn't grow—he remained at the size he started.

In the gym, my friends and I laughed at Mark's routine, but he would just shake his head. He didn't want to lose his swing, he protested. After our workouts, I would be blown out and sweaty; Mark, on the other hand, looked as if he hadn't worked out at all. He remained normal for his size, 6'5", at 230 pounds. I was in the gym with Mark, and I know that Canseco lied about him. Had Mark been using steroids regularly at that time and on any type of training regimen, he would have been growing. He wasn't. At the very least—with little exercise—he would have put on weight from water retention or lean muscle, 10 to 15 pounds or so. But his weight hovered at 230 pounds for years. Over the course of a steroid cycle, you'll see some change. For Mark, there was no change whatsoever. Besides that, Mark didn't even know how to work out properly! You simply don't do a cycle and hope the steroids work without a serious program behind it. He says his use in '89 was isolated, and his body development—or lack thereof—backs him up.

In 1990 the A's continued to be a juggernaut. Mark remained a major part of the machine with 39 home runs and 110 RBIs. The A's cruised through the regular season and then past the Red Sox in the ALCS to reach the World Series for the third consecutive season. The Cincinnati Reds were the newest David to the heavily favored A's.

Dennis Eckersley had once again been the bullpen horse with 48 saves, and Bob Welch had 27 wins. Rickey Henderson ran wild on the bases; Jose Canseco hit 37 homers. They acquired more talent in the form of Willie McGee and Harold Baines. If anything, this A's team looked even better than they had in the previous two seasons. Mark thought they were headed to their second consecutive world championship. But as they say, that's why they play the games. The A's took it on the chin and were swept in four straight games to the Reds. Jose Rijo won the MVP award, and the "Nasty Boys" bullpen of Rob Dibble, Norm Charlton, and Randy Myers dominated A's hitters in the upset.

While the A's fell from their lofty perch that fall, Dan found a place among college football's elite during his senior season at San Diego State. Dan looked like Darth Vader standing in the pocket and staring out at opposing defenses through a dark visor attached to his helmet. Everything he threw seemed to find a receiver that season, and the numbers looked that way, too. He threw for 3,883 yards and 27 touchdowns.

Prior to the season, Dan had packed on about 20 pounds to his 6'8" frame to put him at about 240. The extra size and strength paid off. Not only could he absorb a hit without going down, but he gained speed and arm strength. He lifted three times a week. In addition, he employed anatomical stretching—a practice that helped loosen his hips to make them more flexible—and plyometrics. When Dan wasn't in the gym, he ran running drills. That summer, he worked on his throwing skills, footwork, and quickness. Following a program outlined by David Ohton, SDSU's strength and conditioning coach, Dan became a much quicker 240-pounder. "He's going to set a new standard and style for quarterbacks in the NFL," said Ohton.

The hard work paid off. In 1991, he was selected by the Seattle Seahawks as the 16th pick overall in the NFL draft. He was the first quarterback selected in the draft and 17 picks ahead of Brett Favre, whom the Atlanta Falcons drafted in the second round with the 33rd pick.

Mark was excited for Dan and hoping for the best in the NFL. Mark constantly counseled Dan about keeping his head held high regardless of what happened. He wanted to prepare Dan for that next-level attitude required in the big leagues.

After a year living with the Bonadonas, I moved to my own place in Alameda. I'd learned a lot living with the family, especially about working hard. I'd always worked hard in sports and with my lifting, but I learned responsibility and service with them. Getting up early and not training first thing was an adjustment for me. But it helped me prepare for normal life. Also, I wasn't spending my money, I was working for it. All of it had been a rewarding experience for me at 20 years old.

Having my own place felt good. The place itself had a cool design—I guess you'd call it a studio apartment with a loft. It was my own little bachelor pad. Alas, soon after finding my own freedom, I was back to my partying ways.

Being out on my own, my mind began to wander to sports. Had I given football all that I had to give? I had the size and the athleticism, but I had chucked it all. I had been a pretty good player at Claremont High. Guys in the gym talked about how strong I was—and I was only 21 at the time. I was looking for something, and going back to college and playing a game I had once been good at was it. They inspired me to consider enrolling at a junior college and going out for football; my parents and the Bonadonas agreed. They encouraged me to see if I really had given the sport my all. I decided that if I performed well and wasn't hindered by my eyesight, I would consider taking it to the university level. That thought began to percolate in my mind while I continued to lift weights—steroid free—and make strides in the weight room, even if the amount of weight I could lift had dipped a little without pharmaceutical help.

Finally, I decided to enroll at Chabot Junior College in Hayward, California. I realized that not liking classes had been the major contributing factor for me abandoning football. A couple of years older, I decided that going back to school again would be worth it if I could play football, the sport I had once loved.

In the fall of 1991, I quit the carpet-cleaning business and began making the 20-minute drive from where I lived to Chabot. I still had about $50,000 left from my eye money to sustain me. After enrolling, I looked up the football coach and told him I wanted to play. Standing 6'3", 250 pounds, I expected an open-arm reception. I was wrong. Being the coach of a junior college, I'm sure he'd seen the story repeat itself time and again. It didn't matter if I was chiseled, he understood a basic truth of football: nothing happens until you put on the pads. He wasn't going to do any cartwheels until he saw whether or not I could play.

I went out for the team ready to prove myself, and once I put on the pads, I played well. Even though I hadn't played in two years, I still had it. I quickly gained recognition for being the strongest player on the team as well as one of its hardest hitters. I had pretty good speed for my size—I ran 4.7 in the 40. People made a big deal out of me because I was a McGwire. Everybody knew Mark, and Dan was increasingly gaining fame with the Seahawks.

As the season began, everything was going well, until a couple of games into the season when I found myself on a kickoff return team that I shouldn't have been on, given my blind side. I wasn't thinking about the downside when I tore down the field ready to lay a big hit on some sap on the other team. Kickoff return coverage is wild. I was running full speed, blocking for the ball carrier. There I was, ready to put a tremendous lick on the player right in front of me when—wham!—I got hammered from the right side, the side where I have no vision. All I remember is seeing a helmet come into view. I couldn't react; I couldn't do anything. We collided. He popped me on the right jaw, and I got knocked straight on my butt.

Typical guys being guys, everyone on the team let out a collective groan followed by laughter. They couldn't believe I got laid out like that. My jaw felt like it had been relocated to the other side of my face. Suddenly everything felt weird and out of focus. I couldn't go back into the game. I thought my jaw was broken. Afterward, I couldn't bite down without experiencing a lot of pain. Turned out my jaw wasn't broken, but it remained sensitive for weeks. The experience was humbling.

After a month of going to practice and participating on the sidelines, I tried to return to the field. Once I finally felt like I was ready to hit somebody, I snapped on my chinstrap and went back on the field. Unfortunately, nothing changed. Whenever I hit someone my jaw throbbed. Every hit put me in pain. I was conflicted. I wanted to play football, but the pain was excruciating. I tried changing up the way I hit people. I tried to adjust my technique any which way. But there was no getting around the fact that if I was going to hit somebody on the football field, I had to put my helmet on them. I knew I had the ability to play the game, even at a more advanced level, but I had a huge blind spot. Even if the jaw pain subsided, my vision would always be impaired. It was a liability. Anyone on the field could sneak up on me, and I would be unprotected. Given those factors, I gave up football with a heavy heart.

Football was supposed to be my sport, and leaving the team was an extremely hard thing to do. But I managed to identify some positives. Even though I had welcomed being back in the pads and on the field, I missed the weight room. I really felt that my "thing" in life was to be stronger and bigger than everyone else. I couldn't be that person when I played football. Right then and there I had what felt like an epiphany, and that realization allowed me to give it up. It was comparable to the feelings I experienced after losing the vision in my right eye. My passion was clearer than ever. Bodybuilding had to be my future. I knew what I had to do, and I made up my mind I would do whatever it took to carve out my destiny in the weight room.

That was it. I quit football, I quit school, and I set my sights on becoming a champion bodybuilder.

chapter | ten

The Passion

The more I worked at the gym, the more serious I became about bodybuilding. But I still had to fill out my frame.

Clarity came to me once football failed to work out. Pursuing a career as a professional bodybuilder made perfect sense to me, and I felt blessed to have identified my life's passion. So many people seem to spend their entire lives looking for the thing that gets them excited, something to get out of bed for first thing in the morning. I may have found that purpose, but I was still an immature kid. Sure, I wanted to be a bodybuilder, but I was still caught up with partying and doing whatever I wanted to in the moment. But deep down I knew I wanted to compete. I knew that I had the body to compete and to win. I worked out hard, just as I'd always done, but my lifestyle was holding me back. There are certain sacrifices that need to be made in order to become a successful bodybuilder, and I hadn't made them yet.

Including a lot of protein in my diet was a no-brainer. Most anybody who has ever touched a weight knows that protein is the main agent to get size, strength, and recovery. But there are different carbohydrates and vegetables a bodybuilder needs to eat in preparation for a show. I simply lacked the discipline to be hardcore about my diet. I'd down protein shakes and eat a lot of red meat and chicken, but I also ate pizzas, pasta, and bread. In my mind, I just wanted to get big. I wasn't knowledgeable about dieting properly. And I certainly didn't know how to prepare for being in a bodybuilding show. What I did have was the knowledge about how to lift weights, doing the proper movements, and which exercises would work the different muscles for maximum strength, to become a freak.

On any given night, you could still find me having a few beers with the boys, picking up women, doing shots at the bar, and gorging on late-night pizza or burgers. Eating on the run is a bodybuilding disaster. For me, it was the toughest thing about bodybuilding. Without a proper diet, it's impossible to be a successful competitive bodybuilder. Period.

Mark had a dismal season in 1991, hitting just 22 home runs and 75 RBIs for a .201 average. And after going to the World Series the previous three seasons, the A's finished in fourth place in the seven-team

American League West division. It was a huge disappointment for Mark and for the team.

I suspect that a lot of Mark's problems in 1991 stemmed from off-the-field problems. Mark didn't date in high school, and Kathy was his first serious girlfriend. Shortly after their divorce was finalized, Mark started dating another girl he'd known at USC, and they quickly moved in together. Lacking a lot of experience with women, I think that Mark was ripe for an ambush being fresh out of a failed marriage. I think he allowed her to get in his head, and she kind of messed him up. By 1991, the bloom was off that rose, and his season's performance had his relationship woes written all over it. He had such a horrible year, personally and professionally. I really think the two were inextricably intertwined.

Shortly after the 1991 season, the relationship ended, and Mark decided to make some adjustments in his life. Making adjustments has always been one of his strengths. He learned from his relationship mistakes. He would never again allow himself to be dominated by a woman, let her dictate how he lived his life, or let it affect his career. His life's focus needed to be Mark McGwire. He wouldn't cater to a woman, so if a relationship didn't work out, then too bad. So he made the decision to never consider marriage until after he retired from baseball. And he stuck with it—that's just the way Mark is when he sets his mind to something.

Unencumbered by a romantic relationship, Mark had more free time, which put me more prominently on his radar. He felt bad that my football dream had vanished almost as soon as it began, and he worried about how I was getting along. Early in 1992, I told him I felt burned out cleaning carpets. He asked me to start coming with him to the World Gym in Walnut Creek, where he worked out. He figured it would be a good place for me to work out and maybe get a job there, too.

In general, World Gyms are known to cater to serious bodybuilders, but this particular one in Walnut Creek wasn't specific to that purpose. A lot of big guys worked out there, but it wasn't a typical bodybuilding gym. The owner wasn't a bodybuilder, he was just a business guy who wanted to make some money in the fitness industry. The gym had all kinds of people at all different fitness levels in there. It was a unique place, and Mark really liked it. And they liked having him work out there, too. They treated him really well. Everyone did.

I liked the World Gym instantly, and I made it my home base. And just like Mark said, I was able to get a job there. It didn't pay much, but I sold memberships there, and I made extra cash doing personal training for the members.

Typically, I got my own workout done in the morning and then worked my job in the afternoons and evenings, taking prospective clients on tours through the gym. I didn't really know how to train people, but I knew how to train myself. I knew how to relate my own routines to another athlete, but I had trouble catering a program to a normal person. But I did know the basics. Training beginners, especially women, really expanded my horizons. I started to think about fitness more globally. All in all, working at the World Gym was a rich learning experience—and it was fun. I felt like I was in my element.

Mark lived in Alamo, adjacent to Walnut Creek. A lot of the A's players lived in the area. Oakland has never been a really clean city, so a lot of the players lived in the suburbs, like Walnut Creek, Alamo, Danville, and San Ramon and then made the 25-minute drive into the city and to the Coliseum. After I started spending most of my time at the World Gym, I decided it made sense to get my own place in Walnut Creek.

Even though Mark went to the gym regularly, he still wasn't lifting hard. There was nothing in his program that was serious on his back or legs. He did a little bit of arms and shoulders. In my opinion, it was a wimpy workout. That baseball mentality continued to drag him down: *don't get too big, or you'll ruin your swing.*

Now that I was living in Walnut Creek and spending night and day at the gym, I knew I needed to get back on steroids to reach my bodybuilding goals. I looked forward to reintroducing my body to the juice. I loved taking steroids and the promise of what they could do for me. To me, there wasn't a downside to using them. I'd been off steroids for over two years since I'd moved to the Bay Area, so I didn't have any connections in town. I really didn't know anyone selling the stuff. But I knew at World Gym it would be only a matter of time before I met the right people who could hook me up. All I had to do was establish some relationships. Once I did that, I could ask in confidence if they could get me what I needed. It's really easy to get steroids at the gym. You just get the word out, and it's only a matter of time before it comes back to you.

The more I worked at the gym, the more serious I became about body-building. At the time, I had a pretty good physique. And being big and tall, I grabbed a lot of people's attention. But I still had to fill out my frame. Once I did that, I got a lot more attention from other bodybuilders. "Hey man," they encouraged me, "you can do this." I wasn't ripped yet, but a lot of the serious bodybuilders in the gym could see my potential. They were a great resource. I asked them a lot of questions about bodybuilding competitions, and they told me time and again that I could go a long way. I can't tell you how many times I'd hear, "You get set up on the right program, and you can go really far." Constantly getting that encouragement helped me build the resolve I needed and convinced me that I could achieve what I wanted. I could compete. But I was shy about it. What normal guy wouldn't be? The prospect of standing on stage in front of a large audience wearing nothing but a Speedo was daunting for me. It was a huge adjustment to go from a football player to a bodybuilder, from dominating people on the football field—in full pads and gear, no less—to putting on a tiny bathing suit.

In any bodybuilding competition, the winner is the person who shows no weaknesses on his body. So I started evaluating the areas of my body where I most needed to show improvement. I looked at my body and asked the other bodybuilders around to help me identify my weaknesses. There were plenty of people around who competed and were an invaluable resource. They critiqued me like a judge at a show would, and they explained what those judges were looking for. The prognosis was clear: I needed to build up my chest. My wide shoulders were out of proportion with my chest, so I needed to do more dumbbell work to bring out my pecs. My calves and my lower back also needed attention.

Chest and calves are stubborn areas for me, so I had to work diligently to improve them. But I was committed to making it happen. The seasoned bodybuilders in the gym also advised me on the substances I needed to supplement my workouts, specifically steroids and growth hormones. "You just stay on the program, and you're going to do well," they said. Everyone was telling me how much it would help me, that it would take me to the highest professional level, where I could earn a good living doing what I loved. I think that's why I went a little nuts on them, ultimately.

When we worked out, Mark and I were like ships passing in the night. Plus, my workouts took a lot longer than his, so he'd only be there for a fraction of the time I was lifting. There were times when we finished our workouts at the same time and grabbed lunch or hung out afterward, but it didn't happen often. Mark always seemed to have a busy schedule, whether it was meeting a friend or doing something for the team. But I loved spending time with him when I could, and I think he did, too.

Going out with Mark was always fun. Part of that came from the fact that the older I got, the more I looked like him. We didn't look alike when we were growing up. Sometimes people commented that I couldn't be Mark's brother because I was just too big. I always got a kick out of that. One thing was certain: whenever I went out with Mark, we got a lot of attention. My friends and I loved it. We were like an entourage. Whenever we walked into a room with Mark, people always swarmed to our table like bees to honey. Sometimes I just marveled at the scene and what star power and the smell of money do to people. And Mark wasn't even a superstar back then! He was just well-known in Oakland.

Mark had always been concerned about me, ever since we were kids. That never changed. He was a brother who would always look out for me. He saw how aimless I became after my injury, saw me wandering around, and tried to help. He seemed happy that I had found in bodybuilding something I liked to do and goals that I wanted to achieve. I didn't ask him if he had an opinion on steroids, and he never offered one. He did understand what I had to do to get to the competitive level because he knew the bodybuilder's lifestyle. Hanging out in the gym, you're bound to meet bodybuilders. And talking about steroids wasn't taboo back then, especially for bodybuilders. People in the gym knew who took steroids and who didn't, and nobody passed judgment. It was simply part of the deal.

I visited Claremont to see some friends from time to time, and on one of those visits to Southern California, I ran into a friend, Kristy, whom I had known since the seventh grade. We started dating, and ultimately she moved up to the Bay Area, and we got a place together in San Ramon. It was there that she earned the dubious distinction of becoming the first girlfriend to experience the insecurity of "'Roid Rage" Jay. Just before she moved up, I made a connection at the World Gym. He wasn't a big-time supplier, but he was able to get me a few things. I started on Clenbuterol, a fat burner kind of like fen-phen; Winstrol, which helps get rid of fat and gets you ripped; and a little Testoviron, which helps promote building muscle. Having my hands on them exhilarated me since I knew the power they carried. I wanted more.

Once I started to use again, I went on and off the juice based on my supplier. I needed more than my guy could give me. The funny thing is that it wouldn't have mattered what he'd gotten me—I didn't have the knowledge I needed to get myself into the appropriate condition I needed to be in for a show. I weighed about 270 at the time, but I was sloppy. I'd never dieted in my life, and my body fat told the story. I had more of a football lineman's physique, by no means pure muscle.

While I might have been inconsistent in my steroid program, I was plenty consistent with partying. Unfortunately, that combination hindered me from making any strides at improving my body. In the long term, alcohol inhibits the muscle tissue's ability to grow, killing muscle tissue and creating body fat. Of course, I wasn't thinking about that when I was out drinking. I didn't know what the effects were. But I knew that I was frustrated at not getting the kind of gains I wanted to get in the gym—at least to the point at which I felt confident enough to enter a competition. If you had asked me at that time, I would have told you that entering a competition was my goal. Only time passed, and I hadn't signed up for a single one. All the bravado about becoming a competitive bodybuilder began to sound like idle chatter. I began to have doubts about whether I'd ever follow through with my goal.

In addition to being unable to commit to doing a show, my personal life was a mess. Kristy and I broke up, and she moved out. Everything was her fault, of course. I write that with great sarcasm, knowing in hindsight how screwed up I was back then.

A disturbing pattern took hold in my life and played itself out over and over. I was so selfish, in addition to raging with steroids throughout my system, that I was emotionally abusive to every woman with whom I was involved. My behavior was erratic and selfish, which stemmed from my insecurity. My emotions were raw. If I didn't get my way, I would get angry and lash out screaming. At times, I even physically pushed them around. These were women who cared about me. Some even loved me, but in the long term, they came to think of me as a psycho. They knew I had a good heart and that steroids were causing a lot of my problems, but they couldn't get me to see it. Steroids disabled me emotionally. I never felt secure with myself, which seems odd in hindsight, since I looked like the Hulk, and my goal was to get huge. I have to believe my emotional unrest—the agitation, the irrationality, the cruelty—was a direct byproduct of steroids.

After Kristy moved out, I moved in with my buddy John at a house we rented in Pleasanton. John and I had met at the World Gym and became good friends. Mark liked him, too. We all went out and partied together many times.

Talk about odd couples, though—John and I were a regular Oscar and Felix. John was a power lifter and I was a bodybuilder. And he was natural, while I was on the sauce. Power lifters have a different way of training than bodybuilders. A single lift is what it's all about for a power lifter—and that's what they train for, that one rep. I didn't really learn anything from him about technique, because our goals were in opposition. I'd already learned the basics, anyway. But I respected the fact that he was clean and didn't want to take steroids. It's funny to me now, how I could respect what he chose to do, but I didn't consider how it applied to me. I couldn't see the big picture. I took for granted that I needed to take steroids to advance. I thought that without steroids, I wasn't going to get to a professional level.

John was a strong guy at 210 pounds. He had a good bench, a really good squat, and a great dead lift. Even though I respected his path, I tried a couple times to convince him to try mine. I always told him that if he got on steroids, he could be one seriously strong dude. But he wanted to be known as a natural power lifter. He said it was "his thing." So I left him alone. Despite our differing styles, we got along well. And I appreciated the fact he didn't pass judgment on me. He knew that in bodybuilding you had to be saucing. It was possible to be natural and competing with guys who were taking drugs as a power lifter, but as a professional bodybuilder, that was a no-go.

For all intents and purposes, there is no testing in bodybuilding. There are natural bodybuilding shows that do require testing, but even at those, officials only examine urine, not blood, so it's easy to beat that test with blockers. The urine blocker probenecid and some diuretics do the trick. It's especially effective on oral steroids, which clear from the body a lot faster—anywhere from two to four weeks before testing. Heavy testosterone injectables are more difficult to mask; a blood test will show elevated levels. But blood tests are much more expensive to run and as a result are less prevalent. The professional circuit had no testing requirements. Even if they had, the professionals know exactly what to do to beat them. Pro bodybuilders are more knowledgeable than most doctors when it comes to each and every steroid, HGH, and insulin hormone used in the body. When you start playing with your body's chemistry, you become a scientist. Your timing is precise. You know when to take a certain substance, how much of it to take, how the body will react to it, and when to give your body a rest. As a professional bodybuilder, you're taking these drugs for a living. It's experience that doctors can never have. Some of the more seasoned ones might have 20-plus years of steroid use under their belts. I know a few of them who are retired, and they still look good and healthy. I can't speak to their emotional state.

Arnold Schwarzenegger retired because he knew the effects of long-term use would likely be detrimental to his health. So he parlayed his physique into an acting career and became Hollywood's stud action star. He competed as a bodybuilder in the 1960s through the 1970s, a time when no one was equipped to test athletes. At the beginning, nobody really knew much about steroids and the possible side effects. But I truly believe we wouldn't know who Arnold Schwarzenegger is today if it hadn't been for his use of steroids. He would never have been a champion bodybuilder, Mr. Olympia, or then, of course, a box office star and politician.

In the bodybuilding and wrestling world, the fans love the huge, freaky competitors. That circus is what sells tickets. I remember one year in the late '80s, Mr. Olympia announced drug testing for its entrants. That year, the contestants were smaller across the board. And furthermore, they didn't sell many tickets. It was a weak year for them. The following year they reverted to a no-test policy, and the show saw an increase in ticket sales—not to mention an increase in the size of the competitors. It's what the fans want. And it's just the same in wrestling. Hollywood has made huge money from guys like Schwarzenegger, Stallone, and the Rock. Do you think these guys weren't using in their prime? Who can be certain? The last time I checked, Hollywood doesn't test for steroid use, either. I do know that it cares about the bottom line, though. And the fans will pay. Well, the same holds true with sports. They want to see greatness. They want to see great, larger-than-life figures achieving great, larger-than-life feats—regardless of how they achieve them.

It's no different for women bodybuilders and fitness competitors. Many of the female competitors take testosterones for mass development [Winstrol and Clenbuterol] or a little growth hormone to get lean—a lot of the same stuff the guys take, but in smaller quantities. Many times their usage followed the men's regimen. But for females, the side effects are much more dramatic. In a roundabout way, they turn into a man with all that testosterone going through their blood—growing body hair, sprouting acne…even their periods stop coming. Most disturbing to me, their voices drop. The first time I heard a woman bodybuilder talk was at a bodybuilding show in Orange County. When she opened her mouth, out came a voice so baritone it could have belonged to Barry White. That freaked me out. But then she was massive for a woman and bigger than most guys I knew.

*　　*　　*

I decided I didn't want to work for a while, so I quit my job at World Gym and supported myself on my eye money again. I also struck up another relationship. Lisa had been a natural bodybuilder, and we met at the World Gym, where she worked as a personal trainer. She was older than me and she liked bodybuilders. We started off as friends but then started dating and eventually moved in together.

Lisa's influence helped me finally make a commitment to compete in my first show. We attended the 1993 Contra Costa Bodybuilding Show, which is held in the valley area of Walnut Creek. For anyone competing in the San Francisco Bay area, the Contra Costa is the number-one show to enter. Somehow, watching that show brought everything into focus. That's when everything finally clicked. I made myself a promise that I would compete in that show the following year, 1994. I looked at it as a personal challenge: I had a year to put everything I had into training for that 1994 show. Winning the Contra Costa Show would be a major first step toward becoming a professional bodybuilder, a process that required a series of progressions. The Contra Costa Show is an amateur show, so if I won, a trophy would be the reward; there was no cash prize. But winning there could help me get to a national contest like Mr. USA or the Nationals. Once a bodybuilder wins a national title, he gets a pro card and can compete for money. That's what I wanted, money—a sustainable career as a bodybuilder.

I really stepped up my regimen to the next level and didn't look back. My philosophy was, *I'll do whatever it takes to get me into that shape.* Having Lisa aboard helped me face facts. She knew what I really needed to do to get into the shape I needed to be in to compete, and she didn't mince words. She helped me with any number of things, but accountability came first. She had competed before and knew the kind of discipline that it needed— discipline that I didn't have, that she showed me how to get. She also understood the many mood swings of a bodybuilder, as well as how hard it is to diet while doing all that cardio stuff.

Above all, her encouragement was her top contribution—having her there, supporting me. Not to mention that she just got it—the lifestyle, priorities, mind-set of a bodybuilder, and baggage that goes along with it. She came into my life at a perfect time. She was there the whole way, through the training, the dieting, and all of the crazy things a bodybuilder does to prepare for a show.

On a practical level, Lisa enabled my pursuit. The dogged pursuit of becoming an established bodybuilder served as my compass. I wasn't working, but Lisa continued to work as a personal trainer. She had a good, steady paycheck, and she basically took care of me. I still had my settlement money, but I was spending that on steroids whenever I could get my hands on them. I still lacked that "good connection" that I needed to find. That part of my training regimen was inconsistent, which I knew all too well.

I lifted the weights hard and tried to regulate my diet, but I hadn't run into anyone who could help me get ready for a show. I was still in limbo. I wasn't doing steroids for a lot of that time. My connection at World Gym had run dry, and I felt like I needed help. During this period, I changed gyms, moving to Gold's Gym in Walnut Creek. I had worked out at Gold's Gyms in Southern California, and they had a reputation for being a little more hardcore. As a "serious bodybuilder," which I considered myself, I preferred the hardcore gyms to the fancy ones. In addition to those considerations, I also figured I had a better chance of establishing a steroids connection among a more hardcore set of lifters. While I worked out, I sniffed the room for possible prospects. I was frustrated. After nine months of training for the Contra Costa, I still had no connection to put me over the top. I decided that if I wasn't able to find somebody to help me in time for the '94 show, I'd put it off another year. And with that, I put myself right back into limbo again.

chapter | eleven

The Hookup

I weighed 270 pounds and had 20 percent body fat. Seven weeks later, I weighed 211 and had reduced my body fat to 2 percent. Not only that, but in doing so, I managed to keep all of my muscle. It was only then that I got a true idea of how muscular I was, and could be.

An early chapter in my life as a McGwire brother: Mark holding me as an infant, alongside my brother Dan.

Mark and me in 1973, at the Tournament of Roses Parade.

The McGwire 1976 family photo: (clockwise from left) Bob, Mike, Dad, Mark, Dan, Mom, and me.

The 1980 Claremont Athletics, like many things, were a McGwire family affair. Check out my dad (back row, right), Dan (second row, far right), and me (front row, fourth from left).

The McGwire 1982 family photo: (clockwise from back left) Dan, Bob, Mike, me, Mark, Dad, and Mom.

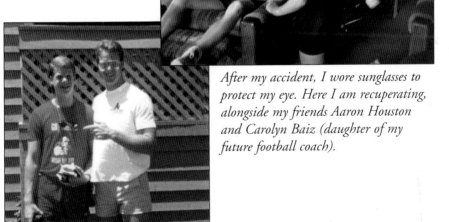

After my accident, I wore sunglasses to protect my eye. Here I am recuperating, alongside my friends Aaron Houston and Carolyn Baiz (daughter of my future football coach).

Visiting Mark at Class-A Modesto.

I started pumping iron more seriously after my accident.

I was six feet tall at age 15 but no stringbean. The results of my lifting were evident early on.

My first bodybuilding competition, the 1994 Contra Costa. I won the heavyweight and overall divisions.

Me at my hugest, during the 1996 Contra Costa competition.

At Mark's house before the '96 Contra Costa. This is both of us at our peak condition. Even at my biggest, I never had forearms as big as Mark's! No wonder they called him "Popeye."

Mark in 1988 (top) and 1996 (left). Canseco claims my brother was juicing in '88, but there's no way. Look at the difference in his physique in 1996, at the end of his steroids run. Both his arms and legs tell the story.

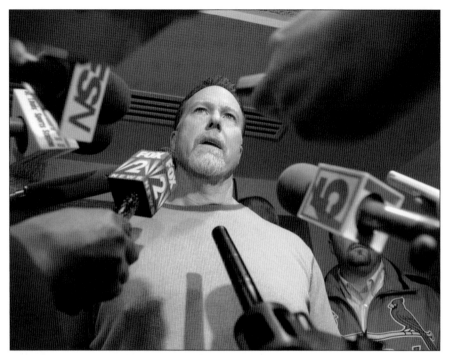

After nine years out of baseball—and the public eye—Mark meets the press.

My family (left to right) McKenzie, Eric, Francine, and Brooke.

My diligence to find a steroids connection finally paid off in February 1994 when I met a guy at Gold's Gym in Walnut Creek who had a hookup in Sacramento. This guy had the goods I needed and a reputation for getting people ripped and ready for contest shape. Despite my own best efforts and Lisa's help, I didn't know the details I needed to in order to get myself shredded. I had plenty of muscle, I just didn't know how to amp it up. As it turns out, there's a science to it. You can take all the drugs in the world, but if you don't do them right, they won't work to their best effect—and you're going to lose the contest. So when I went to Sacramento to meet this guy, I felt like I hit the jackpot.

I met him seven weeks before the competition and just said, "Okay, we have to get things going."

Bodybuilding requires an intense sprint to the finish. That seven-week period leading up to a competition is when they are won or lost. My guy was in Sacramento, so I had to travel to him once a week. He competed himself and worked as a trainer, so his base of operations was set up there. I drove to meet with him once a week to get my program set up and to get the drugs I needed. He wrote down my regimen on a piece of paper and handed it to me. It was up to me to muster the discipline to follow his prescription. He wanted to monitor my improvement every week before the contest. He also told me to work out with more reps. He didn't want me lifting heavy anymore. So I added 25 to 30 more reps per set. I was tired. I was on a strict diet, and I was taking in a limited amount of calories per day. My energy tanked easily.

HGH, Clenbuteral, and Winstrol became a part of my regimen for that period; it was a combination that worked well for me. Just taking those drugs and HGH burned an incredible amount of body fat; it just leaned me out. The results can be stunning in conjunction with the right diet and a program of cardiovascular work. I weighed 270 pounds and had 20 percent body fat when I first went to Sacramento. Seven weeks later, I weighed 211 and had reduced my body fat to 2 percent. Not only that, but in doing so,

I managed to keep all of my muscle. The drugs and workouts sucked a lot of the water from my body, and with a diet that practically eliminated carbohydrates altogether, my body fat was reduced staggeringly. It was only then that I got a true idea of how muscular I was, and could be. I was 211 pounds of pure muscle the night before the contest. And I loved it.

Of course, you can't just take the drugs and think you're going to look ripped. You have to do the diet. You have to put the time in, do the cardio, and follow the workout program. It's hard work and incredibly difficult, but to me it was worth it.

The diet could best be described as static. Three times a day I ate eight ounces of halibut fish and a cup of broccoli or other green vegetable. Other veggies weren't allowed. Carrots have a little sugar in them, so they were off limits since my mission was to completely deplete my body of sugar and carbohydrates in order to burn up all the body fat. Once in a while, I'd switch to grilled chicken, but I ate mostly fish because it was a leaner protein. Besides, grilled chicken is really dry; I had to sprinkle a little lemon pepper on it just to add a little flavor to get it down. In between meals I drank protein shakes—but not your run-of-the-mill, Jamba Juice variety. The protein shakes I had didn't contain one carbohydrate or speck of sugar. They were just straight whey protein. It wasn't much fuel for all the physical exertion I went through in a day, but that was precisely the idea. I was consuming the bare minimum of fuel that I needed to get me through.

My day began at 7:00 AM with 45 minutes of cardiovascular exercise followed by an hour of weights. The workouts are a little bit different during the period leading up to a big contest. Instead of working to build a lot of muscle, the goal is to add definition to the bulk of the muscles you've already created. So I used lighter weights and repped out every set with four sets of each movement. The number of movements varied by the area of the body I worked on a given day. In a week-long program, I'd devote one full day to my chest, shoulders, legs, back, or arms, and two days out of the week I'd work my abs.

In the afternoon, I tried to rest and eat; then I'd head back to the gym at 10:00 PM to do another 45 minutes of cardio before going to bed at 11:30. Heading to bed so quickly after a workout helped me to burn calories at a high rate while I slept. I'd be back with the same routine the next morning. The key to any diet is to burn more calories that you put in every day. If you do this, your body will eat up the excess body fat in time.

It takes a *mentally* strong person to do this day after day, but it works. My body began to operate like a well-oiled machine. My metabolism felt like a blast furnace. I'd feed the fire a little bit of fuel, then the weightlifting and cardio I did helped me burn fat all day long. I ate just enough protein to keep from losing muscle. It was tough work, and I was plenty cranky day after day, but it was paying dividends physically.

I had my eyes on the prize. All I thought about was the upcoming show and about how I was going to conquer there. It was the only way I could get through that routine day to day, but I set my mind to it. I didn't look ahead more than a day. I wanted to look good for my first show, and I wanted to win. Winning that contest meant everything to me. I had attached my future to its outcome. If I could win the amateur show, I could move up the amateur ranks and ultimately become a professional body-builder. I knew I had the required discipline inside of me. In fact, I think it's something that all of my brothers share. Mark definitely has it. We get it from our dad. But those seven weeks of training required more discipline than I could have ever imagined. It forced me to reach inside of myself to find untapped reserves. There were plenty of temptations in those final weeks before a show, but I remained vigilant.

I started to crave any and all carbohydrates. When you deny yourself carbs, your body goes nuts. I wanted sugar as if my life depended on it. I cheated by eating one small breadstick a few times, and they tasted like candy to me. Coffee became my dessert—black coffee with Equal. Caffeine gave me quick energy because my body was so depleted. It was an incredible taste, especially since it was my only break from fish and broccoli.

Life had to go on even though I was training, which meant going to a restaurant from time to time, and that was a trial. There is nothing more difficult than denying yourself that pleasure in a place where everyone is enjoying their own culinary delights.

Watching TV, it seemed like every commercial was about food. Talk about Pavlovian—on a diet of nothing but halibut and broccoli, seeing a Whopper or pizza on the screen nearly made me cry. I was literally salivating at what came across the screen. Driving past a barbecue restaurant was torture. People talking about food made me want to leave the room. I felt my stomach barking at me constantly.

I would have given my right arm for a slice of pepperoni pizza—okay, several slices with a few ice-cold beers. There were countless times when I felt like caving, but I dug deep for the mental toughness to move past such cravings.

At the end of a day of dieting, lifting, and cardio, I felt spent. That was a tough time. I had limited energy. Holding a job would have been extremely difficult. Living with Lisa and having some of my eye money leftover enabled me to pursue my goal full time. I might not have been working, but bodybuilding was my job. I have known bodybuilders who have held down jobs while they have trained and competed. I find that remarkable. Those guys had to be nuts! But it reinforces my belief that bodybuilders are the toughest, hardest-working people in the world. The fact that they take steroids doesn't invalidate that. Everyone takes them, so the playing field is even. But being a successful bodybuilder, someone who wins competitions, takes a mentally strong attitude because that person also has the perseverance to follow a diet properly and do all of the necessary cardio work. For me, that cardio work was perhaps the biggest test, particularly the final cardio workout of the day.

After eating so little, I felt depleted when I reached the final cardio hurdle of the day. I find cardio work boring, so I switched it up—usually between Stairmaster, treadmill, and the stationary bike but sometimes other activities. The basic idea is to keep moving and keep your heart rate steady for a long duration at a certain pace. My target heart rate zone was calculated by the following equation: 220 – age (23 yrs.) = 197 x 70% output = 138 beats a min. Keeping that level for 45 minutes will burn the leftover body fat on your frame. Not only were the cardio workouts boring, they were completely draining. More often than not, I got shaky or lightheaded during those cardio workouts. Forty-five minutes is an eternity when you're tired, bored, and starved.

Finally, at the end of the day, I spent about 15 minutes practicing posing. It may sound like a cool down, but posing—flexing your muscles—is a workout in itself. In competition, you must hold each pose for 10 seconds, then go directly into another pose, then another one, and so on. It's a tiring pursuit.

While the training brought so many challenges to conquer mentally, getting prepared for the actual show brought out challenges I would have never considered. For starters, the whole thing about wearing a Speedo in front of an audience made me uneasy. I mean, I'd never worn a Speedo. I'd made jokes about guys who wore Speedos my entire life. Europeans wear Speedos. Eventually I got so big and ripped that I got over that fear.

I'd spent my whole life lifting weights, but I didn't know anything about posing. It's an art in and of itself. My supplier/trainer worked with me, and Lisa—who had been in shows and knew how to pose—was invaluable. They also helped me put my music together. I'll admit that I had some issues to get over. Moving around to music simply didn't seem "manly" to me. My thoughts turned to figure skating and the high-pitched voices of Olympic champions describing triple axels and pirouettes. But I knew I had to get past those associations—it's what I had to do if I wanted to compete. I chose Van Halen's "Right Now"—about the furthest thing away from the Ice Capades I could think of.

Flexing the right muscles during a pose wasn't nearly as easy as I thought it would be. I spent a lot of time in the mirror practicing all of the different poses required. As the competition crept ever closer, seeing myself change in that mirror was the reward for all my hard work. Staring back at me I saw a shredded, ripped body that I felt proud of creating. I almost couldn't believe how I looked.

The day before the competition, the plan called for me to go completely carbohydrate free. I had nothing but straight protein. My brother Dan was in town to watch me compete, and Lisa and I took him to a Mexican restaurant for dinner. By that time, going to restaurants didn't faze me in the least. You could have piled every temptation in the world in front of me, and I would not have dared compromise myself. I felt jacked about the contest. I'd worked so hard to get there, and the adrenaline was coursing through my veins. I felt exhilarated just thinking about what was to come.

I'll never forget that dinner. We were waiting at a table in the back of the restaurant for Dan to arrive. He hadn't seen me in a while, so I was excited for him to see "the new me." I'll admit, I looked completely different. Looking at my face, someone might have thought I was sick or something. I literally had no fat or water in my face. I was sucked down completely at that point, dry as a bone. So when Dan entered the restaurant, I stood and waved at him to join us at our table. He looked at me blankly, with no recognition whatsoever. I started walking toward him, and he still didn't recognize me. Finally I spoke: "Dan, it's me." He did a double take and said, "No way! Look at you." I couldn't have been prouder.

Later that night I showed him how ripped I was underneath my shirt, and he just stared in disbelief at my chiseled frame. Dan always had been one of my biggest supporters, so I was thrilled that he was there to see me compete. It was special spending the night before my big day with him.

During that seven-week stretch up until the night before the contest, I'd been depleting my body of carbohydrates. And during the final days before the competition, my diet was straight protein. It was crucial to monitor my electrolyte intake in order to avoid body cramps. When the body is depleted of water, it is incredibly vulnerable. It's a very dangerous state to be in, eliminating one's water intake. I took a number of mineral capsules. The night before a contest, everything flips, and you get to carb up. I didn't go hog wild at the restaurant, but as soon as we got home, I went straight for the yams.

A normal person may not get too excited about eating yams, but at that point, I wasn't a normal person. I'd turned into a lean machine. I had followed my program to the last detail, and I was shredded. But I was also depleted of carbs and subsisting on the least amount of water I could take in. When I ate those yams, they were a complete shock to my system. It was almost as if I was on drugs, it felt so good. Suddenly I had boundless energy, just from eating a few yams.

Taking in carbs before the contest is calculated—it'll make your veins pop out noticeably. Putting glycogen back in your body is straight energy for your muscles. The last-minute carbs make you look fuller and not so sucked down—you fill out about five pounds or so. Drinking a little water—just a tiny bit, like sucking on ice cubes—makes those veins come right out.

Looking in the mirror, I still couldn't believe my eyes. The finishing touches to my pre-contest regimen gave me the look I wanted. I'd followed everything to a T and couldn't help but feel that all of my hard work and sacrifice were going to pay off.

As it was, my body couldn't have been in better shape for the contest. Still, there were things that I needed to do. A couple of days before the contest, I shaved my entire body. Participants do not want to show hair on their bodies in competition; a hairless body is the best way to show off the definition of the muscles. I'd shaved my body a lot in the past, but I had held off shaving for a while to ensure that my skin would be totally smooth for the contest.

After shaving, I began the process of darkening my skin. I'm a fair-skinned guy, so it was a dramatic change for me. In the old days of bodybuilding, competitors with light skin used iodine to simulate a tan. My method was a more-than-liberal application of Pro Tan, an instant tanning spray favored by bodybuilders and swimsuit models. By the time I finally got the color to where I needed it to be, I'd applied nine coats of the stuff. I was really dark.

Even though I felt confident when my head hit the pillow, I was nervous and excited about the contest. A lot of who I was and who I wanted to be was attached to the outcome of the contest. I wanted to win. It was all I wanted, all I worked for. Of course, all that worrying wasn't going to change how I performed the next day, but my mind was racing.

Even so, I was ready.

My whole family came to watch the competition, except for Mark, who was nursing yet another injury. I felt bad for him. Physically, he just seemed to be breaking down. In 1993, he had played in just 27 games because of an injury to his left heel. Ironically enough, even when Mark missed time on the baseball field, the statisticians managed to find some significance in his accomplishments. His nine home runs in 1993 were the second-most hit by a player who had 100 or fewer at-bats during a season. Ted Williams established the record of 13 homers in 91 at-bats in 1953.

Mark underwent surgery in Houston in late September 1993 to repair a partial tear of the fascia in his left heel. In addition, he had a small bone spur in the same foot that was shaved down. He went to spring training in 1994 fully healed, but he quickly went out of action again. A stiff back caused him to miss the first three weeks of exhibition games. He returned to the A's lineup in time for Opening Day, but by the end of April—and the time of the Contra Costa competition—he was on the disabled list with a stress fracture in his left heel.

The contest was held in Antioch, California, at an old theater that held about 2,000 people. There were two portions of the contest. Prejudging took place in midmorning. During that phase, all the contestants in the same weight class took the stage together—for me, that meant the heavyweight class. I didn't know what to expect. The judges were all seated there, and they called out what pose to strike. They called out things like, "Give me a front double biceps," and all of us followed suit by doing our best double-biceps pose. Or "Give me an abs shot or a back shot," and we'd choose our best. That night, the part of the show that is performed on stage in front of an audience is the more exciting part of the competition. But from what I understood, the prejudging is usually the portion where contests are won or lost.

I didn't feel very nervous for the prejudging half—I think because I didn't feel as self-conscious with only a handful of judges watching and a few spectators, trainers, and friends in the audience. Most of the people who were there were well educated on the sport. Not to mention, all of the competitors in my class were on stage with me at the same time. It was a far cry from what would come later that night. For one thing, my whole family would be at the contest that night. What if I caught a glimpse of them and started cracking up? What if I simply felt too self-conscious to go out on the stage once my name was called? After all, I was just wearing a tiny bathing suit!

Looking around at the rest of the field, I felt good about my chances. Sure, there were some good guys in the contest, but I had spent the last years of my life living and breathing this sport. I knew what to look for—and what to look like. I just felt that I was a little bigger than everyone else, in addition to being more balanced and leaner. The prejudging felt like a breeze.

Posing to music was the first part of the nighttime show. Just as I had done prior to prejudging, I did a little lifting before going out on stage. The key is not to do too much. If you get too much blood in the muscles, you lose definition. It was another example where following the encouragement of Lisa and my trainer's advice paid off for me. I did a few reps with light weights, some push-ups, sit-ups, stretches, arm curls, and triceps presses— just enough to get a little blood in there and get the veins coming out. My veins were already popped out because I was so lean. By lifting just a little bit, the blood rushed to my veins and made them stick out dramatically.

Taking the stage for the first time meant fighting off a river of anxiety. When they called my name, I was anxious. My legs felt heavy, like I had to trudge through ankle-deep mud just to reach the stage. It was all I could do just to make it onto the stage without tripping over my own two feet. Fortunately, I made it to the stage, and the music started playing. Having everybody in the room stare at you and your every movement is a strange feeling—it's completely nerve-wracking. But once the music began, I started to feel comfortable. I started posing, and I could hear the crowd yelling my name. That's when I really started to get into the moment. My posing routine started with the front double biceps pose—designed to highlight arms, abs, and legs development—and the crowd went wild. Then I moved to a side chest pose to show the thickness of my chest, arms, and legs, then to a back double biceps, which revealed my back development, including my butt and hamstrings, all the way down to my calves. A back lat spread showed the width and thickness of the back. Then I turned around to the crowd and did a front lat spread that showed the width and thickness of my back, chest, and legs on full display. Then, I went into my most muscular pose. I flexed my body in a crab position that put my traps, delts, chest, arms, and legs on display. My whole body appeared flexed in a huge, thick, and vein-popping pose. I knew I had crushed it when the crowd went crazy. For the remainder of my routine, I went back and forth into positions that fit the beat of the music, like striking a pose in harmony with a drum beat, which seemed to get the crowd working for me. I smiled and raised my arms to incite the crowd to yell for a big pose, and then I gave it to them. The nerves had left me, and I was having fun by then. It was a high for me just to hear the crowd pump up for me when I posed. What I had dreaded turned out to be an exhilarating experience. Once I was out there on stage, all I wanted to do was stay there. I had put in so much hard work, and in the end, I only had the stage for a few minutes. Talk about glory being a fleeting experience.

I felt like I nailed my individual routine and that the contest was mine to lose heading into the pose off, the grand finale in which each competitor in a weight class takes the stage at the same time. My comfort level had risen dramatically by then. I stood among the other contestants and flexed, giving different poses and listening to the crowd go nuts. The poses were exhausting, but I hardly noticed. Everything I did seemed to be in complete harmony. That night was a singular experience: everything that I had done to prepare, everything that I trained to do, happened just as I had planned it.

Standing on the stage as the winners were announced, I would have been shocked if someone else had been named the winner of the heavyweight division. Happily, that shock never came. I was Jay McGwire, winner of the heavyweight division. My emotions flooded to the surface. Finally, my hard work, my confidence, my goals—they had all been validated.

After the winners of each weight class were announced, they called us out onto the stage to have a pose down for the overall winner in the novice class division. I won the overall weight class, too. Working for something and seeing it come to fruition brought a great sense of accomplishment to me.

I had played sports my entire life and knew what it took to be competitive. Yet winning this particular contest brought me more satisfaction than I'd ever had before. Over the years I'd played in some big games in football and done well, producing some big sacks at crucial times. But something about this contest felt so invigorating. I'd gone through so much agony and sacrifice to get there. And I'd set my mind to do something and went out and did it. To that point in my life, competing in that contest was the hardest thing I'd ever done physically and mentally. And it was something that I achieved as an individual.

Winning that show also furthered my dream. I knew I still had a long way to go to in order to become a professional bodybuilder, but I'd just won my first show! It was the encouragement I needed to keep going. And that was what I thought, out there on that stage: *I'm going to be a pro bodybuilder now. I'll just continue doing what I'm doing, I'll pay my dues, and in three to five years I'd be on top of the bodybuilding world.* After all, I was only days away from my 24th birthday, and I was the winner of the Contra Costa!

Afterward, I met up with my family. They were proud of me—another McGwire achieving excellence. My parents didn't seem to know or understand how I'd swelled to such mammoth muscular proportions. I think they knew what was going on, but we never really talked about it. I didn't feel compelled to tell them. At the time, they seemed happy to see me passionate about something, not to mention succeeding at it.

We celebrated at a Chili's after the contest. Eating that queso dip and salsa might have been the best part about the whole thing. I drank half a beer and felt buzzed—that's how disciplined I had become in my diet. Only a year ago I had been knocking down a case of beer on any given night, while remaining in control. "Jay the Party Machine" had become simply "Jay the Machine." I was disciplined and in control. I was in charge.

I thought about Mark, the only McGwire missing from our party. He was in agony from his injuries yet again. I thought that maybe I could help him. I had the connection. I only needed to convince Mark that I could help him heal. It was like a light bulb went on. Finally, after all those years of Mark helping me, I had found a way that I could return the favor.

chapter | twelve

The Plunge

"You've got nothing to lose, really,"
I told him.

Mark continued to be stubborn. But I
continued to push: "Hey, I'm hooked up,"
I promised. "I have a guy I can trust."

My world was in total harmony after I won the Contra Costa contest my first time out of the gate. Not only did it enable me to continue the journey toward realizing my dream of becoming a professional bodybuilder, it also stirred an insatiable desire inside me: I wanted to help Mark get past his health issues. In essence, he had turned into a broken-down slugger. I knew how to help.

I felt like King Kong sitting atop the Empire State Building. I was powerful, confident, and in control. Meanwhile, Mark's body began to break down. He was looking at the end of his baseball career if his fortunes did not dramatically change. Back and foot injuries had all taken their toll on him. And once again, injured by the midway point of the 1994 season, concerns about his health loomed large. He decided that if he couldn't get healthy enough to return that season, he could be done with baseball.

I think winning the contest earned me Mark's respect. He understood excellence and the price that must be paid in order to achieve it. Mark knew the truth about what I put into my body, but he also understood the other things I did, the amount of sacrifice required to accomplish what I had accomplished.

Ever since I had begun using steroids again, I'd made tremendous gains. Those gains did not go unnoticed by Mark, but the idea of him using steroids never seemed to cross his mind. Mark is a cautious person when it comes to making big decisions. I took it upon myself to convince him of the wholesale benefits he could derive from using steroids. Understanding where he was with his health, and considering the fact that I had established a quality supplier in Sacramento, I just felt that getting him on a program made perfect sense for him. What plan did he have? Continue to break down until he was forced to retire? Steroids had long been used as a way to heal faster. They could help! Besides, he was on the disabled list, so it was the perfect time to start working on his body. "You've got nothing to lose, really," I told him. "Otherwise, you'll need to become an expert at bunting the ball to get on base. That is, if you can run, because you sure won't be able to turn on it," I teased him.

Mark continued to be stubborn. But I continued to push: "Hey, I'm hooked up," I promised. "I have a guy I can trust."

Having someone to trust in the world of steroids is half the battle. The main objective is to buy the good stuff, because there's a lot of junk out there. Because of the demand as well as the lack of regulation, there are a lot of crappy products out there, a lot of fake stuff. So finding a reliable connection, someone who could supply the good stuff, is a huge advantage. Money can be an issue with some people, since the truly good stuff costs plenty, but it wasn't going to be an issue for Mark.

I told him that Deca Durabolin could make a huge impact on his health. I described what a powerful healing agent it could be and how taking it could soothe his barking tendons. Deca is a phenomenal drug that gets into your joints and makes you feel great. Mark seemed to ache all over back then. To anybody in such pain, the prospect of taking any kind of drug to help the healing had to be extremely attractive. I could understand his dilemma—it was why I wanted to help him! There he was, a devastating home-run hitter throughout his career, and he was about to end his career in baseball at age 31. I asked him if Major League Baseball had steroid testing; I honestly didn't know whether they did or not at the time. He told me there was no steroids policy because the Players Union had declined to collectively bargain for it. By the union's way of thinking, drug testing qualified as a privacy issue, and requiring testing was an abuse of human rights.

My ears perked up. I saw an opening and pounced on it. "How perfect is that?" I said.

See, Mark follows rules; I took it upon myself to convince him that he was well within the right to move forward. If Major League Baseball didn't have a steroids policy, then it's not a violation of the rules. I could sense that he was going to give me the green light. And I think the dam just broke for him, and he realized, *This can be a good opportunity for me.* He was frustrated, struggling, and hurt all the time. The idea that his career could be over had to be everpresent. On top of all that, there I was, his kid brother and the picture of health, whispering in his ear about how phenomenal being on the sauce could be. "Mark, you've got to keep your mind open about doing this," I told him.

I wasn't thinking about the consequences or the prospect that it could change baseball history. We weren't trying to create a home-run machine that would threaten the legacy of Roger Maris and his single-season home-run mark that had stood the test of time. All I could think of was how much I wanted to help heal my brother. I thought about all of the times Mark had helped me. I was grateful to him for everything he'd done, and I still looked up to him as my big brother. I sincerely felt that helping him heal his body and build it up properly would be one of the best things I could do for him.

Still, Mark was never the kind of person who would jump right into something. He's extremely cautious. I had to convince, convince, convince him until he finally broke. I told him how good I felt, that I trained with heavy iron all the time, and my elbows didn't hurt a bit. My shoulders didn't hurt, nor did my lower back. In fact, nothing hurt. "This stuff is really going to help repair you," I said. "When you work out, you're going to be sore, but you're also going to recover twice as fast."

Somewhere in the course of a conversation between brothers, baseball history was changed. I know that he wouldn't have considered using the stuff if he wasn't injured. I was the one who convinced him to do it. Mark wouldn't trust anyone else. My heart told me that I was simply trying to help a brother in need.

In addition to the healing prospects I saw ahead for Mark, I saw in him a blank canvas. I pictured what a beast he could become with the proper training, and I wanted to use my expertise to help create a masterpiece. And I thought of the possible combinations that would serve him best. Deca Duroblin was perfect for him since it would strengthen and help his tendons and muscles while allowing his body to heal faster. In short, it is the perfect recovery drug. Combining growth hormone with the Deca would get him leaner and increase his appetite so that he could put a lot of good calories into his body. That would, in turn, promote lean muscle mass. I liked the way that combination sounded in my mind and thought I knew the right recipe. I trusted my Sacramento connection and wanted his added expertise. After all, it was his program that got me to the victory circle at the Contra Costa Bodybuilding Championship. Why couldn't he help lead Mark to a productive major league career?

I accompanied Mark to Sacramento, where we met with my supplier and trainer, who explained to Mark how the different drugs would work on his body and answered myriad questions. I think the two of them connected and that Mark trusted the guy. After all, the supplier was even more of an expert on steroids and the growth hormone—and especially dosages—than I was. I had experience taking steroids, but this guy had been in programs like this for years as a competitive bodybuilder, not to mention all of the people to whom he prescribed. Much of what I learned over the years was directly from him. Mark asked a ton of questions and had a litany of concerns typical of a beginner.

In Jose Canseco's book *Juiced*, he writes about injecting Mark with steroids in bathroom stalls at the ballpark. He claims that Mark took steroids with him in 1988, after his rookie season. Mark wasn't into weight lifting that much back then—and he didn't display any physical manifestations of steroids. And why would Mark take any drugs after the awesome year he had in 1987 with 49 home runs? It just doesn't add up.

Then, when Mark first tried steroids for a few weeks in 1989, he expected results. Obviously he had no idea what he was doing! Steroids are long-term drugs. There's no way to get the benefits without putting in the time and doing the work. When I approached him in 1994, he was very naïve. He had no experience with steroids, no idea which was which or what worked with what. He didn't know anything. Mark is a very practical person. He consistently checks all the angles and makes any decision with caution. It's just his nature. Letting his teammate inject him with something he didn't know about or understand just doesn't make sense at all. Not to mention that the notion of Mark and Jose fitting into one of those tiny bathroom stalls at the Oakland Coliseum is ludicrous. It would have been like squeezing two elephants into a phone booth. Besides, you do the injecting at home—not in a public place like the ballpark.

I helped start him on the stuff in 1994. I had started educating him about steroids, and he knew nothing. I was an open user, and I was his brother. There were no regulations against it in Major League Baseball.

Mark wasn't juicing with Canseco. Looking at pictures of Mark's body back in 1988, when Jose claimed to be shooting his butt full of steroids, anyone can see that he doesn't show any discernable bulk. Jose got ripped, but Mark remained lanky. Take a look at his legs, arms, and shoulders in 1988—then fast-forward to 1996—and you'll see what I'm talking about.

When he agreed to consider taking steroids, he advanced carefully. Even though I knew a lot about steroids, I had to say, "I don't want you to take my word for it. I want you to meet the guy that I'm connected with so he can explain everything and what the benefits are." It was only then that he said yes.

My connection and I agreed about the program Mark should get on. We both advised him to take low dosages. For someone like Mark, he didn't need to inject a bunch of steroids and get immediately huge. Adding too much bulk in a short period of time would have affected his swing. Any gains needed to be made gradually, so we mapped a program that ensured that he wouldn't turn into the Hulk overnight. Mark listened studiously to everything we told him and asked a multitude of questions. He wanted to know everything there was to know about steroids before he put them in his body. The three of us sat down and discussed the benefits and drawbacks of the various steroids he could take and determined what we should get Mark on. We talked about dosages, quantities, and techniques. We talked and talked exhaustively, but finally, once he did his due diligence to the point where he felt comfortable, Mark told my Sacramento connection and me that he was ready to start the program.

A week or two later, my Sacramento guy hand-delivered the goods to Walnut Creek. The program was HGH and Deca for about four months to start. The biggest benefits an athlete gets from using HGH are its anabolic effects on the connective tissue within muscles and an increase in lean muscle. Fat loss and lean mass increases with HGH, so Mark used a dosage of two and worked up to four insulin units every other day. In addition, he used 300 to 400 mgs of Deca a week.

Mark didn't like shots, so he favored the oral steroids over the injectables whenever it was possible. Like most first-timers, he didn't want to plunge in the needle himself. I was the first person to inject him. If I wasn't around, one of his girlfriends would do it. You might think that was really some kind of dramatic moment, but it wasn't. As a steroid user, it's a clinical thing, just like getting a shot from the doctor. You use the same insulin needles used by diabetics for the HGH and regular syringes for the thick, oil-based testosterones. The insulin needles are very thin, so it's possible to inject yourself in the stomach like a diabetic if you want. The problem is, if you're not careful where you stick yourself, you'll start to develop scar tissue. To avoid that, it's best to choose a fleshy spot, like the deltoid, hip, or glutes.

Growth hormone is administered with an insulin needle and measured by insulin units (ius), whereas the dosage measurement for a regular needle is in ccs, or cubic centimeters. To inject yourself with a regular needle, as you would with steroids like Deca, the hip or shoulder is the best area.

Since Mark was injured when we started, he wasn't traveling with the A's. Instead, he just committed himself to working hard in the gym. I became his personal trainer, and we did the very basic movements: heavy weights with reps, forced reps with assistance, and core stuff—lower stomach, back, and legs. The aim was to strengthen his core, so that when he turned on the ball it would generate a lot of power. We were careful with the squats because of his history of back problems, so we did leg presses and leg extensions to strengthen his legs. The body's core, the area from the top of the abdominals to the top of the knees, is the most vital area to strengthen for success in any sport.

We isolated each muscle belly on his frame. Lifting through a half range shortens up the muscle belly. We wanted to elongate the muscle belly, so we did sets of full-range reps. A muscle is just like a rubber band. That's why you want to go for a full-range stretch: to become more flexible when weightlifting. Weight resistance with full-range movements enhances your strength, balance, and flexibility. The myth in baseball is that having muscles will slow you down. That can be true if you don't know what you're doing. But we knew what we were doing. And Mark became more flexible at 260 pounds at his peak in 1996 than he was at 230 pounds in his early years. He remained flexible, quick, and strong with the bat because we trained him gradually and guided him properly to maintain his flexibility. His bat speed increased incredibly due to his gains in strength and flexibility, and his power went through the roof.

We had him do basic movements for the pectorals, including the bench press with dumbbells and barbells, including weighted flys for flexibility. The rep counts were high in the beginning of his training—we did 15 to 20-plus reps for each set. We never went heavy with the weights on his chest. Too much mass development in the chest would have restricted mobility in his swing. For his shoulders (deltoids), he did side, front, and rear laterals with dumbbells and cable motions to develop and strengthen his shoulders. He did dumbbell and barbell shrugs to develop his trapezoids. We did all the movements when we came to the arms. For biceps, we did barbell and dumbbell or cable curls, standing or sitting on a incline bench, or preacher curls, where your arms are over the pad to isolate the bicep with a barbell or dumbbell, as well as hammer curls with dumbbells to build the forearms connected to the bicep.

For the triceps, the program called for cable extension pushdowns, dumbbell presses behind the head, barbell presses and barbell extensions on the bench, and overhead cable extensions with a rope or bar. These movements were always controlled, and there were always a lot of reps built in to increase his endurance.

Feeling the burn on the way down and the way up (a strictly controlled negative and positive range of motion to all movements of the body) for each movement makes you really feel the lactic acid build up in each muscle belly. It causes an awesome pump to whatever muscle you're working on, especially the arms. Mark's forearm workout was awesome. He did wrist curls off his knees sitting down and reverse wrist curls with weights of upwards of 100-plus pounds with 30 reps. He also did ropes, slowly twisting the rope with a weight dangling from the bottom of the rope and twisting the rope up and down with his hands until it burned so much he could no longer do it.

We didn't do too many dead lifts because of Mark's lower-back issues. Instead, we focused more on hyperextensions to get isolation on his back muscles. To accomplish that, we used lighter weights and stretches. To develop the lats, we did wide- and close-gripped pull-downs, one-arm dumbbell rows, incline dumbbell rows, and cable low rows. In addition, we incorporated hammer strength equipment for one arm and pull-back movements for both arms to increase his width and increase strength in his upper and lower back.

Mark couldn't and wouldn't do squats because of his lower back, but we did plenty of leg presses. Leg presses are safer because the back is supported against a padded seat. He did leg extensions for the quads and numerous leg curls—seated, lying, and standing—to build up that hamstring. He stiff-leg deadlifted with light weight to get the full stretch in the hamstring. To imagine what those are like, it's basically like bending over to touch your toes with a barbell or dumbells in your hands and holding it until you feel the burning stretch, after which you come up with it and go back down again. But that exercise really stretches the hamstring and increases flexibility dramatically. As a result, you are far less likely to pull a hamstring, a common injury for athletes when they run. That flexibility allowed him to get that big body of his moving when he needed to run. He eventually got to over 600 pounds with reps of 20 or more in his leg presses, a monster amount for a baseball player. Considering the before and after pictures shows a significant difference. It was in his legs where Mark's power really took hold, and he was able to turn on that ball in the batter's box. He had built up a huge reservoir of leg strength. Combined with 19-plus-inch guns and 17-inch forearms, he started to hit bombs that didn't just clear the wall, they cleared the wall by significant distances.

Mark's calf workout was pretty basic: standing calf raises as well as doing the sitting motion with good weight and holding that weight for a good stretch in his Achilles tendon really burned that muscle from the back of the heels to the top of the calves. We isolated Mark's abs with full-range sit-ups and short, tight crunches; super settled with leg raises; and worked side-to-side raises to hit those obliques in order to get a full-range stretch and contraction on the movement. We also applied heavy-resisted, ab-weighted machine crunches.

I knew from my years of weight training that the muscle really strengthens and grows when you push it to the max. And by the maximum, I mean past failure and beyond. I truly believe that this is why a lot of people don't get the results they're looking for. If you go to the gym looking to work out, but you don't have a plan or a program established, then all you're doing is guessing. With all that guesswork, the results end up fairly limited. People who lift weights but have no form and technique, whether they do the bench press, squats, or anything else, won't get results without consistency and precision. Technique should be a lifter's top priority. It's true of any sport. It was a lesson my dad taught us as kids. Without swinging the golf club properly and making sure that clubhead comes down flat to the golf ball, you'll hook or slice the ball. The same thing applies in baseball. If Mark hadn't always possessed the technique to get that bat around to connect squarely with the ball, you would never have heard of him. He never would have made it to the major leagues, much less the minors.

Possessing good technique in weight lifting means that you can't do half-range motions on the bench press, or in squats, arm curls, triceps extensions, pull-ups, or anything else. When the bar doesn't touch your chest doing bench press, you're only working out the front of your shoulders and triceps—you're not even really working your chest muscles. The whole idea for the bench press is to gain strength and development for the chest muscles, but without a full range of motion on the exercise, there is zero isolation of the muscle. And without isolation, the muscle can't really be broken down and penetrated, and without penetration, the muscle won't grow.

It's the forced reps (full-range reps) that make the muscle burn, which causes the muscles to grow. The next day, you'll feel sore because of the microtears that happen in the muscle, a side effect to breaking down the muscle. Proteins (amino acids) are crucial for muscle recovery. The amino acids will heal those microtears naturally in six or seven days. With steroids, that recovery would take three to four days at the most. It is a big reason why steroids are so popular and attractive to the athlete and bodybuilder alike. Because testosterone increases protein synthesis, it's the process in which cells build proteins. It makes the recovery process so much quicker.

The hardcore style of training we used with Mark dated back to the Schwarzenegger days and carried an element of danger with it. Any time you push your workout to the max, there is a possibility for injury. These kinds of workouts used to make me throw up. For example, I did squats with 405 pounds for 10 reps, and then my partner would force me to do 10 more reps—20 reps for the set was a huge number, and it made me throw up. I loved it though. I'm sick, I know. But I had no fear in the gym.

For Mark's workout, the program started with a warm-up with a moderate weight, just a couple of sets to get the blood flow increased in that muscle. Then, with a spotter like me or my trainer/supplier (we both trained Mark), we put a good amount of weight on the bar or dumbbells and had him do the full-range reps, a method known as the shock-the-muscle method. When Mark burned out on the reps, I forced him to do more reps to really feel the burn, stretch, and contraction of that muscle—in bodybuilding circles, they're known as "force reps" or a "total burnout set." The key is to increase the weight every set and keep the reps the same (15 to 20 reps with a spotter), so that each set becomes more challenging. The muscle reacts by gaining durability over time. The exercise creates muscle density, thickness, strength, endurance, and flexibility. Mark's results and his success in the gym came down to the workouts. Without the right training program, it really doesn't matter what else you do. Your results are limited if you are doing things wrong, steroids or no steroids.

Of course, there are injury risks. It's easy to pull or tear a muscle, so you have to know what you're doing. Between each set you must stretch out the muscle. After four to five sets, you need to move on to the next movement, doing four to five different movements for each muscle group.

Mark didn't diet like me. But then, he wasn't trying to get bodybuilder-ripped either. But he did begin to eat quality carbohydrates instead of poor carbs or refined sugar. Quality carbs for energy (in moderation) are any fruits (simple carbs, for quick energy), oatmeal, potatoes, yams, brown rice, wheat germ, wheat bread, pastas, bran cereal, any grains (complex carbs, for slow-burning energy) and all vegetables (enzymes, to help with digestion). In addition, he was loading up on protein. It's tough to go wrong with protein—steak, chicken, fish, eggs, turkey, ham and protein drinks are all great (unless the meat is fried). He began eating every three hours. We went to restaurants like Outback, Black Angus, and the Hungry Hunter Steakhouse and ordered two filet mignons for dinner with either red potatoes or rice with veggies and just inhaled our food.

Sometimes in the morning, a couple of hours before we worked out, we went to a waffle place in Danville and loaded up on waffles, pancakes, or oatmeal and a half-dozen eggs each. It didn't matter if we carbed up before or after our workouts; as long as we just ate good-burning food (fuel) that the body could easily break down for energy, we were golden. Mark needed at least a gram to a gram and a half of protein per pound of his body weight to fuel his muscles to enhance his recovery and muscle growth. And we always needed the calories because our workouts were brutal.

On drugs and HGH, the need to put food into the body is everpresent. Mark was always hungry, and I told him, "This is why you're going to put lean muscle mass on your frame. The HGH and the workouts are going to increase your appetite and metabolism. Your muscles require more calories because they are constantly burning body fat and food all day long." Bottom line: muscle burns fat tissue. "Muscle is the greatest natural fat burner that God made," I'd tell him.

I had steered Mark onto the road he needed to travel to get back into the game. I felt good about helping him achieve his goals, and he felt good about the prospect of staying on the field, helping his team, and collecting a nice paycheck.

I think if Mark had not gotten hurt in 1993 and 1994, he never would have taken my advice on the steroids, HGH, and the training program. He wouldn't have needed it by his own reasoning—and I certainly wouldn't have tried to convince him. I think he would have been content to be a 30-plus home-run hitter every year. Only he did get injured, so we'll never know what might have been.

chapter | thirteen

The Resurgence

Despite the strike-shortened schedule that year and the 33 games he missed in two stints on the disabled list, Mark finished with 39 home runs in just 317 at-bats. In addition, his average home-run distance was 418 feet, which led the major leagues. You could say Mark McGwire was back.

Over the course of the 1993 and 1994 seasons, Mark hit just 18 home runs—a total that had once been considered a good two-month period for my brother.

The 1994 season ended with yet another surgery to Mark's left heel. His first surgery had been performed in September 1993 to release the medial part of the fascia in his foot. The season-ending surgery in August 1994 was performed to release the lateral aspect of the fascia. Mark had been literally falling apart in front of my eyes. Understandably, there were a lot of people who believed baseball had seen the end of Big Mac. But those critics just didn't know what had been taking place in the Walnut Creek Gold's Gym while he was away from the game.

Mark was out of baseball in late 1994, but then so was everyone else. On August 12, 1994, the players followed through with what they threatened to do if their demands were not met in the new labor deal and they walked off the job. The player's strike absolutely crippled baseball, and neither side seemed willing to budge an inch. The lack of compromise resulted in baseball commissioner Bud Selig's September 14 declaration that the remainder of the 1994 season, including the World Series, was cancelled.

The strike caused teams to lose approximately $600 million in revenues, and its players lost $230 million in salaries. But that paled in comparison to the loss felt by the fans of the game. "How in the world could these greedy players and owners not reach some middle ground?" they groused. Fans were dumbstruck by both sides and heartbroken at the cancellation of the World Series, perhaps the most venerable of all sports traditions. It was revealed during the free-for-all that the average major leaguer's salary stood at $1.2 million a year. As a result, the players took the brunt of the heat from the fans. It was a sad time for baseball, on all sides.

After my successful showing at the Contra Costa show, I was more determined than ever to continue moving forward with a career in bodybuilding. I knew that I would find stiffer competition in the 1995

Contra Costa Championship, since I had moved up from the novice class to the open class. The men in the open class were experienced body-builders who had already won a novice show. If I could win an open show, I would qualify to compete in a national show. And if I could win a national show, like Mr. USA or the Nationals, I would turn pro. The path was right there in front of me. So I redoubled my efforts and looked toward the future.

Normally, after competing in a show, I would add a lot of weight and bulk up during the off-season before cutting it all down again in the 2½-month period before my next show. But after the 1994 Contra Costa show, I decided to stay lean. I continued to use drugs, but I wasn't doing a lot of them. The main reason was that I discovered that I liked being lean. That was the first time I'd ever been that lean in my life. I looked great and felt great. Taking my shirt off and being that lean but thick is a good feeling. I didn't want my body fat to get any higher than 10 percent. I kept a clean diet and did more cardio. What can I say? My vanity won out.

Lisa and I were getting along and still living together, but I eventually became very jealous. I started to break her down emotionally. Mark never liked Lisa because he thought she was too old for me. He thought that she took advantage of me and that I couldn't handle her. But the problem wasn't what Mark thought. My steroid usage was adversely affecting my emotional well-being. I began to party a lot—drinking and doing steroids at the same time. It was a toxic combination, and having the two substances coursing through my body made me aggressive. I'm sure I provoked a lot of fights I wouldn't have otherwise.

Lifting weights can give you a huge amount of energy. It can also inflate your ego. I loved that feeling so much that I never wanted to get off steroids, even though I'd learned on day one that you need to cycle off to give the body a break. But I felt so much strength and confidence that steroids became the center of my world. I saw bodybuilders in magazines and on

ESPN, and I knew most of them were using steroids. They made me look like a child, they were on so much stuff. I wanted to be the biggest, strongest bodybuilder out there and become a professional, and I knew I couldn't do it without steroids.

I was already inherently aggressive, but the steroids really made me rage. I could be cool with the people that I hung out with, buddies that I worked out with or partied with, but if I ever caught an awkward glance from anyone I didn't know, if they were sizing me up, I could blow up at them. I would be yelling and screaming in 2.2 seconds—over nothing! You feel like Bruce Banner as he's flying into a rage and turning into the Hulk. Steroids just did that to me.

Fortunately, nothing ever really happened though because everybody always backed down. I think no one wanted to challenge me because of my size. It's common sense. Nobody wants to try to start something with a defensive NFL lineman, do they? Well, that's the size they were looking at when they saw me fill up a doorway. My mind-set back then was that if anybody did want to throw down with me, I could have easily kicked his butt, and not just because of my size, either. When you're pumped full of steroids like I was, you have an attitude that you can kick anybody's butt at any time. Your mind-set is that of a conqueror, a warrior. I was like Lyle Alzado, John Matuszak, and Bill Romanowski—all three of them NFL players who were simply raging animals. Steroids are powerful, and they alter your attitude. They make you feel invincible. I would do anything and everything to win any battle put before me.

My problems with Lisa started to escalate, and I began to consider moving out of her apartment. Fortunately, Mark was aware of our issues, and he offered to help me. He also thought I could help him by moving into his house. He liked the idea of having someone live there when he wasn't there. But mostly I think he wanted to help his kid brother, the one who always seemed to have a world of problems. I moved into Mark's house at the end of 1994.

Since I relocated to the Bay Area, I had been closer to Mark than we were even as kids. And now that I had him on a program and lived under his roof, we became even closer.

Mark lived in Alamo, California, in a custom house with a sweet backyard that had a rock pool. The house sat perched on a little hill, and the backyard had an amazing view of the other hills, where custom houses were spread out everywhere. It was the good life, no doubt about it.

We certainly weren't living complicated lives during that time. We worked out together, went out to eat frequently, and sat around chatting, mostly about girls and working out. Mark had a cast on his foot for a little while after the surgery, but that didn't stop him from working hard. Getting back to the top in his profession meant everything to him. He'd been hurt for a long time, so he wanted to go to camp in the spring of 1995 and show everyone that he was in the best shape of his career.

Even while he was still in a cast, Mark began to feel better. It's what steroids and growth hormone do for you. You feel great and get stronger. Your body begins to heal at a record pace. Mark's chemical program helped him heal quickly and allowed him to work out harder. But he still had to put forth the effort—and did he ever. He impressed me with the way he went after it in the gym. And I'm a tough critic.

I knew he always had that work ethic in him. He'd shown me that when I was a kid with the gusto put forth in every sport. The workouts we designed for him weren't all about size. The primary focus was to keep him healthy while getting him leaner and growing moderate muscle tissue. So the drug usage and the workouts were a scaled-down version of the extreme versions bodybuilders like me would follow. He saw the dramatic effect on me, and that wasn't what he wanted. He could have gotten as huge as me, maybe bigger. But his focus was on getting healthy and active.

I had great confidence it would work. In my mind, the desired results would be just a matter of time. There's a formula for success, and that program, used properly, produces results time and again. I can build anybody up to be the size of an ox or in the best shape of his or her life, if asked to. It's all about putting your effort in, taking the right supplements, and eating the right foods. It's about keeping constant discipline. Even without drugs, you're going to see lean muscle mass on your frame within six months.

Mark worked out a minimum of five days a week for about an hour and a half each day. He did cardio on top of that to stay lean, again a scaled-down version of the intensive program I did. Mark believed in putting away the baseball equipment in the off-season. A lot of players have batting cages at home and work tirelessly all winter at honing their stroke. Not Mark. He didn't take batting practice during the off-season. He didn't even want to talk about baseball. Then again, I guess that is understandable, given the fact that every professional baseball player eats, sleeps, and breathes baseball nine months out of the year. Mark did stretch to remain flexible, and he swung the bat in the garage occasionally once spring training began to approach.

In the off-season, we trained hard during the day and we partied hard at night. Mark loved to go out to dinner and so did I. The only time we cooked was when we barbecued with friends. But mostly we'd go out, eat a nice meal, and then hit the scene. It might sound superficial, but when you're in your 20s and you're treated like a rock star because you are with your brother who can hit a baseball a mile, I'm here to tell you life is rich. And I was more than happy to take full advantage of the preferential treatment accorded me because I was with Mark.

Mark drank vodka, Stoli, straight up. People always thought he was drinking water. One of our favorite spots was an Irish pub in Walnut Creek called Crogan's. By the time we got there, people would be lined up down the street waiting to get inside the place—but we never waited. They would open the doors for Big Mac, his kid brother, and whomever else. We walked right in like we were out of *Goodfellas* or something. Every now and then we'd get a comment from a different kind of wiseguy. I remember one time when some guys in the parking lot recognized Mark in his Mercedes Benz and said, "Hey Mark, the way you're playing, you should be driving a Toyota." Mark just laughed. Criticism from other people never bothered him. He understood that in life, you have to take the good with the bad. I know that the criticisms just fueled him to keep training hard. After all, those are the same fans who praised him endlessly when he started producing again.

Sometimes we'd venture to San Jose to a huge country nightclub called Saddle Rack. They had bull riding, three different stage bands, and a dentist chair used for purposes quite unlike those my father used in his practice. They would recline you back in that chair and dump hard liquor down your throat. Driving all the way to San Jose might have seemed extreme, but the women were worth it. They were all just gorgeous there. And as soon as anyone heard that Mark McGwire had stepped into the joint, every eye in the place was looking at us. It's hard to miss us because of our size. That was the great thing about hanging out with Mark: you didn't have to hunt for girls, they would just come to you. Not to mention plenty of those girls mistook me for Mark...but I never exploited that situation, of course!

I remember one occasion when the Yankees were in town. Mark had some friends on the team, so after their day game, he rented a limousine shuttle for a bunch of the guys, and there was a waitress along who served us drinks. We partied all day and all night. Later that weekend, we met a bunch of Yankees players in San Francisco at a place called Johnny Love's and had another wild time.

Partying with celebrities is really cool, especially when you're 24 years old and buffed. The treatment you get by just hanging out with the celebrities is unbelievable. You feel like royalty. And it wasn't just the girls who mobbed Mark. The guys, fans, wouldn't leave Mark alone. They all wanted to be his new best friend. One of the reasons why Mark liked going out with me and my buffed friends was so we could protect him from overbearing guys like that. We looked like a bunch of bodyguards, anyway. And we were all on steroids, most of us. We would close places down at 2:00 in the morning and people would hang around outside to talk to Mark and get his autograph. It was nuts.

We had a good time during that off-season, and a lot was due to how good Mark felt. The cast was off his foot, and he'd been on the program for a while. He started to get an idea about what he might be able to do when he reported to play baseball in 1995—*if* the players went back to work.

The strike stretched into the beginning of 1995 with no end in sight. If anybody understood the power of the Players Union and what that power meant for salaries and other benefits, it was Mark. After all, under the current system, he had advanced to the point where he stood to make $6.925 million to play baseball in 1995. That figure made him the sixth-highest-paid player in the game. Mark felt strongly that the current players had to pay their dues, even if it meant having to stay on strike, in order to make the system right for the current players as well as those who would play in the future. He completely trusted the players who worked with the Players Union to negotiate the best agreement with the owners.

Using replacement players for spring training and regular-season games became a hot topic early in 1995, and baseball's executive council approved the idea of using them on January 13. Once the plan was put into action, it seemed as if any player who had ever thrown a baseball or swung a bat came crawling out of the woodwork. Selig gave the plan his blessing by telling anyone who cared to listen that the owners were committed to playing the 1995 season "with the best players willing to play."

Mark considered the idea of using replacement players a joke. And even if the fans were mad at the players, he believed that no self-respecting baseball fan would watch a major league game under such a mockery. He wasn't alone. Sparky Anderson refused to manage the Detroit Tigers if they used replacement players and was granted a leave of absence. Baltimore Orioles owner Peter Angelos declared that he wouldn't use replacement players, and the Maryland House of Delegates passed legislation that barred teams using replacement players from playing at Camden Yards. And the Toronto Blue Jays planned to play their regular-season home games at their spring training home in Dunedin, Florida, due to Canadian laws prohibiting the use of replacement labor during a strike or lockout.

The baseball strike disgusted most people. Nobody wanted to see his or her heroes wearing sandwich boards and standing in a picket line. Finally, on April 2, 1995—a date that coincided with the originally scheduled start date of the season before it was delayed by ongoing negotiations—the strike finally ended after 232 days.

The season was shortened to 144 games, or 18 fewer than a normal season. Players and owners alike would find that the shortened season would be the least of their problems. The strike had disheartened fans. Suddenly, stadiums that normally would have been overflowing with spectators were half full. Many of those who did buy tickets were malcontents who booed the players and owners for disrupting America's national pastime. Television ratings suffered as well. Baseball needed a hero.

Cal Ripken Jr., whose pursuit of Lou Gehrig's record for the most consecutive games played, was one of the players who helped bring the fans back. But the timing was also right for a revolution within the game. Fans liked seeing home runs; the owners agreed. And pretty soon players who hit the long ball began to take the spotlight. Most people didn't ask why it started to happen. Those who did figured the balls were juiced, the parks were smaller, and the pitching was in a bad state due to the addition of expansion teams that diluted the talent pool.

Mark stepped back into this atmosphere in 1995 fully equipped to be baseball's next hero. Mark had perfect timing to become a piece in the perfect storm to make baseball a great and exciting game to watch again—

bombs away! There's nothing more exciting than seeing a baseball leaving the yard. Of course, Mark had no idea at the time that he would be one of the heroic figures who helped revive the game of baseball. He just felt excited about being healthy again.

By the time Mark headed to Arizona for spring training in 1995, he had more muscle tone and yet leaner muscles than he'd ever had in the past. And yet we'd still managed to hang about 15 pounds of quality weight on his frame, bringing him up to 245 pounds. In addition to the gains he'd made in his physique, he brimmed with confidence.

Mark's extra confidence proved invaluable. Strength can be a crucial ingredient when trying to beat someone who is trying to strike you out. Mark has never been a guy to get very excited about anything, but he was excited about having his new body to show off in camp. And he was eager to see what he could do on the field thanks to his new and improved body. Sure enough, they were impressed. And for the next two seasons, he would arrive at spring training bigger than when he had finished the previous season.

Later that year, we introduced him to other drugs for the next couple of years during the offseason, D-bol (oral, 50 up to 70mgs/day), Winstrol (oral, 50 up to 80mgs every other day), and Primobolan (oral, 60 up to 80mgs/day) for a minimum of 12 weeks. These are mild dosages to a body-builder. I almost double these dosages in my program and I would use way more testosterone injectables. We rotated these drugs and stacked them. For example, Deca works well with Primobolan, which makes for a great stack that promotes lean, strong muscles.

Mark made the lion's share of his strides in the weight room primarily during the off-season, since it is more difficult to get to the gym consistently during the season. Once baseball began in the spring, he did just enough to keep his muscles hard and the blood flowing. He saved the hard training for the fall and winter.

Some friends and I visited him in Arizona in the spring of 1995 before the A's started playing their exhibition games, and his behavior showed me how much he had changed. Fitness had become a major part of his life. He'd practice with the team early in the morning. When he finished at noon, we'd go right to the gym. He had bought into the program! I was all for it. Besides, I needed to work out since the 1995 Contra Costa Show was just around the corner. I didn't need to cut as much weight as I did in the previous season since I stayed fairly lean, but I still needed to get the reps. After we worked out, we went tanning and then grabbed lunch. We'd rest a little bit and then go out in Scottsdale at night.

Since Mark was a well-known athlete, he was afforded all the trimmings of being a celebrity. Once, we were pulled over in Scottsdale for speeding. Mark gave the officer his driver's license, and the policeman went back to his car to run the name and the license plate. When he returned, he handed Mark his license and said, "Slow down, Mark, and have a good day." Mark got away with it. He always did. Even I got preferential treatment because I was his brother. People loved Mark and made a big deal over him. And it always seemed to make him a little bit uncomfortable. He never liked talking about baseball when he was away from the field—and I didn't blame him. He always preferred the women who had no idea who he was. He'd invariably be disappointed when they found out right away that he played in the major leagues. Once they found that out, they got clingy fast—his number-one turnoff. Mark liked women who liked him for who he was, not what he did.

Early in the 1995 season, Mark had a career-high 18-game hitting streak from May 3 to May 24. On June 10, he had his first multiple-home-run game of the season when he hit a pair against Boston. The following day, Mark hit three. The five home runs he hit in two games tied the major league record that he already shared. Despite the shortened schedule that year and the 33 games he missed in two stints on the disabled list, Mark finished with 39 home runs in just 317 at-bats. In addition, the average distance for one of Mark's home runs was 418 feet, which led the major leagues. You could say Mark McGwire was back.

During the season, it's really hard to get to the gym, but he wanted to do enough lifting to keep his muscles hard and keep the blood flowing to them. He did his own thing, which meant working out, but he couldn't do the forced reps by himself. It's a different workout when you have a trainer in your face. But Mark definitely had been converted. He believed more than ever in the benefits of weight training, and he wanted to keep himself big and strong, so he lifted after the games. That way he'd get in a good workout and he'd also avoid the media. Some reporters would hang around until he finished, but the extra time after the game usually culled the crowd of reporters wanting to talk to him.

Mark's body had changed drastically, but he also made changes to his game. After sitting around for most of the previous two seasons, he was able to observe and study the game carefully, taking time to watch the different pitchers' strategies and also study opposing hitters. In the past, he'd been a guess hitter. After deliberating, he decided that was the wrong approach. In 1995, his approach became "see the ball, hit the ball." That concept was born from studying how the opposing pitchers went about their business.

After the games, when he lay in bed at night, he visualized the pitches that would come from the following night's opposing pitcher. After working with batting coach Doug Rader, he still stood in that pigeon-toed crouch when he stepped into the batter's box, but he altered the release of his swing, dropping his top hand and allowing for a one-handed follow-through.

I derived a great deal of satisfaction out of seeing Mark succeed in 1995. I was happy for him and felt as though I had done something to help out my big brother when he needed it. My parents were even caught up in what I had done for Mark. They thanked me for helping him with his weight training. I got a lot of the credit for Mark's improvement, but nobody was talking about whether or not Mark had received some chemical assistance. They all assumed he had done everything naturally. Everyone was just excited about him returning to baseball and getting back to his home-run stroke.

In the spring of 1995, I came in fourth in the Contra Costa's open class. At a shredded 230 pounds, I wasn't discouraged, since I faced much stiffer competition. But the loss did force me to reconsider the way I did things. After that contest, I decided I would really bulk up and add a ton of muscle. Then I could cut weight when the contest got close. I put all my marbles into the drugs and growth hormone. I ran into another supplier in Walnut Creek, and this guy had it all in bulk quantities. So I bought a year's supply of the stuff. It's staggering how much stuff I had in my possession. And all of it was for me to prepare for the 1996 contest.

That summer, I moved in to Mark's beach house in Newport Beach, in Southern California, near our hometown, Claremont. Talk about living right! Mark's house was right on the boardwalk near Balboa Pier, a location where everyone rollerbladed, biked, ran, and walked. There was always a lot of activity, day and night. Girls were everywhere. I couldn't have imagined a more enticing place to live.

While living there, I worked out at the Club Met-Rx Gym in Cosa Mesa, the town next to Newport Beach. I'd invite some of the guys from the gym over to hang out and enjoy the scenery. We sat on the front patio right next to the boardwalk and barbecued as people went by. Sometimes we sprawled out on the rooftop, where you had the most magnificent view of the beach and the Pacific Ocean. My friends loved that house because of all the action. They never wanted to leave. Me either.

Sometimes we'd walk a block to the little town of Balboa, where the bars and restaurants were located on the Balboa Harbor, where all the boats are. Newport Beach was all about entertainment, food, and girls. Everybody wears swimsuits day and night, and people are just there to have a good time. I got a lot of attention because of my size. I looked like an NFL player. Almost daily, people asked me which NFL team I played for; occasionally I'd tell them.

Aside from all the fun, I still worked hard in the gym. By the end of the summer, I had reached gargantuan proportions, tipping the scale at 320 pounds. In my mind, there would be a lot of added muscle left on my frame once I carved off all the fat and water prior to the contest in the spring.

Because diet is so critical to the program, I always prepared my food ahead of time. All of the serious bodybuilders prepared their food, supplements, and drugs. I cooked chicken, steaks, brown rice, and potatoes in giant quantities two to three days in advance. I carried meals in Tupperware when I anticipated I couldn't get quality food where I was going. Every night I made a stack of pancakes with peanut butter and syrup and ate them before I went to bed. I ate five meals a day and drank two weight-gainer shakes between the meals. Each shake was a whopping 900 calories. My meals consisted of at least three chicken breasts or two steaks and half a loaf of bread, two big potatoes, or a cup of brown rice. In the morning, I would have a cup of oatmeal and eight scrambled eggs for breakfast. I'd set my alarm for 3:00 AM every night to wake up and drink a protein shake. I ate a meal every three hours. The bulk-up phase for any bodybuilder is quite different than the phase two months before competition, eating an 8,000-calorie diet day in and day out.

Mark's second season of intense workouts and steroid use began once the 1995 season finished. He didn't take growth hormone during the season, so the four months in between the seasons were the only times he used HGH. We set up his cycles accordingly. Mark started working hard during the fall of 1995. Again, you just can't put a value on how much harder you will train when you have someone pushing you. His workouts were intense and highly advanced, but they still fell short of the much heavier sets executed by a competitive bodybuilder. He had no need to work out the way I did. If he had, he wouldn't have been 260 pounds, he would have been 280 or more. It might have ruined him.

Mark had always had a special swing that produced home runs. Combining that swing with extra muscle and fitness brought compelling results. Throughout his workouts, we strived to make sure he remained flexible. He did a lot of stretching and core movements. And those were the key to keeping him flexible while adding muscle and strength.

chapter | fourteen

The Crash

Even though I was big and strong,
I felt like I was weak, small, and a loser.
I knew I could get bigger. If only I
could just push it a little further....

Steroids served as my magic elixir for a long time. Considering the way they made me feel and the obvious benefits they gave me, I often wondered why everybody didn't use them. When I looked at myself in the mirror, all I could see was my size. I had worked hard, made a lot of sacrifices, and it had all paid off. I was who I intended to be. Had I looked a little closer, I would have understood what I was doing to myself. Unfortunately, I found out the hard way that steroids were not the answer.

Today I could give anyone a litany of reasons not to use them. Everyone knows the benefits of what steroids can do for you physically: increase your size, strength, and endurance and hasten recovery. But steroids are dangerously addictive, and there are plenty of physical and emotional side effects that come along with the physical gains.

I think all males lean toward aggressiveness. We're naturally protective creatures, and I think we carry a desire to dominate in our genes. These are tendencies enhanced by testosterone, which the human body produces naturally. When a person uses steroids, those testosterone levels skyrocket, thereby intensifying the emotions of aggression and dominance. When I was on the drugs, I was always ready for a fight. I would kick anyone's butt, anytime. I also had a hair-trigger temper. I couldn't control it, but I was blinded by the notion that I was *in control*.

Testosterone is a powerful hormone. Goosing the levels in the body can be extremely dangerous. While I was on the juice, my attitude was completely different. I was powerful, and I knew it. It changed the way I approached everything.

When I first started on the drugs, the shift was imperceptible. But like Sandburg's "Fog," it came on little cat feet, stealthily creeping up on me. I saw myself getting bigger, but mentally I felt the same. It came on quietly, but after a while I was completely changed.

My girlfriends complained that I was too aggressive, too moody. I was uncompromising. Everything was black or white. Messing with hormones, even if you increase just one of them, throws the body's system out of balance. I was operating like a manic depressive. When I was high, I was really, really high. And then I'd crash. On the days that I felt good, I was invincible. I walked into a room and felt like I had a presence, that I was the king.

I saw the same thing happen with Mark. Getting on the sauce made him more confident and aggressive. That I-can-do-anything attitude might not be safe on the streets, but in sports, that's half the battle. Feeling as if you can beat the other guy is a huge competitive advantage. On steroids, that attitude builds and builds until it's the only thing you can see. The downside is that you begin to crave that feeling. You want to feel that way all the time, and you'll do anything to get it. That line slowly starts to blur, and you've lost control. You don't have to think about cycling off of it, because you don't want to get off it. The feeling you get is so satisfying, why would you want it any other way? Maybe deep down you know it's not the real thing. After all, you've never felt that way before. But if it feels good, do it, right? Why mess with a good thing?

I've never taken cocaine or speed, but I've heard from people who have that taking the stuff makes you feel that same kind of high, the kind that makes you want to feel that way forever. Any drug has that potential. Steroids are no different.

Once the drugs took hold, I had a completely false perception of my life. I was often in a state of euphoria. I won't lie—I loved being on steroids. I loved feeling like I was invincible, that whenever I walked into a room I was the A-No.-1 bad dude in the building. I can't speak enough about the confidence steroids produce. It makes a good athlete into a great athlete and a great athlete into a superstar athlete with great confidence.

Unfortunately, when you take synthetic steroids, your own testosterone stops production. A normal person's endorphins are produced and released constantly. When steroids are introduced to the system, the body senses the abundance of endorphins and stops production.

An overabundance of testosterone in the body creates an incredible strain on the liver. Your skins starts to break out, and your blood pressure and cholesterol spike. Prolonged steroid abuse creates severe risk of cardiovascular disease, hair loss, liver damage, gynecomastia, and testicular atrophy.

Your mood starts to fluctuate drastically. One minute you're high and the next you're low. I always tried to regulate my moods by going to the gym, my safe haven. It was a place where I felt safe, where people knew and supported me, but also where I got that burn. When I was there, I could concentrate on what I loved most—bodybuilding—and nobody raised an eyebrow over how I looked or what was happening to my body. I sensed people's approval when I was there. And I just kept growing and growing, blind to how out of control my life had gotten. I'm thinking, *I'm not going to work, I'm going to get my pro card, and I'm going to win. I'm going to be Mr. Olympia.* I was living in a fantasy land.

I should have seen the writing on the wall. Mark came down to Newport after the season was over, and he summarily kicked me out of his beach house. He saw that I was going nowhere. He told me, "Jay, go get a job."

He had seen me competing year after year and watched me burn through all my eye money. He was concerned that the drugs had gotten out of control. Despite the fact that he was on the drugs himself, he could recognize how close I was to going over the edge. He'd seen me get irrational with women; he watched me cruise along without a job. More important, he understood the cold, hard realities of becoming a professional bodybuilder and what I had put myself through in order to achieve that goal.

He wasn't being cruel by sending me packing; he was showing me tough love. He told me, "You have to go home, live with Mom and Dad, get a job, and start thinking about what you're going to do with the rest of your life. You're 25 years old, you have to get off the pot and do something." I moved back home with my parents in October, but I didn't get a job. I continued preparing for the 1996 Contra Costa and Mr. California contests.

In the fall of 1995, I traveled to San Diego with friends to meet my family at Jack Murphy Stadium. Dan played for the Miami Dolphins, who were in town to play the San Diego Chargers. Dan's career hadn't really gone as expected. He had sustained a number of injuries that limited his playing time. He fractured his hip against the Cowboys and then later hurt his throwing wrist. After that, his stock seemed to dwindle with each passing year. In Miami, *another* Dan ran the show, so our Dan didn't see much action. Dan Marino still called the signals for the Dolphins in 1995, but he was nearing retirement. None of us knew then that our Dan was headed in the same direction. It's likely he would have been given a shot at the Dolphins' starting quarterback spot once Marino retired, but I think Dan had just had his fill. He didn't get along with Jimmy Johnson, the Dolphins' head coach. Problems began in the spring when his coach gave him a hard time about traveling back to Seattle for his daughter's birth. That rubbed Dan the wrong way. Johnson wasn't a family guy, he was a football guy. Dan didn't like that. He didn't like being second or third string, either, or the prospect of shuffling around from team to team just to stay in the NFL. After the 1995 season, he hung up his spikes permanently. I still think he retired too early. But I understand why he did it. Dan is a great family man. I think he just wanted to be with his wife and children more than spinning his wheels in the NFL.

Friends and family were tailgating before the San Diego game. When they saw me walking up to them, they couldn't believe the guy they were looking at actually was me. The last time they had seen me had been a year earlier, when I was a very lean 245 pounds. Flash forward to the parking lot at Jack Murphy Stadium: I was 75 pounds heavier, in the midst of the bulking-up period leading up the 1996 Contra Costa contest. They were all astonished. Everybody knew I was juicing. You had to be a fool not to recognize the effects steroids had on me. They didn't confront me about it, but

I did get a few lighthearted remarks like, "Jay, take that syringe out of your butt."

Even though they might have known about them, talking about steroids simply wasn't polite conversation. Back then, people knew about the steroids, but there wasn't the same "evil" perception of them that there is today. It seemed to me that nobody really seemed to care one way or another. In fact, if a bodybuilder had been in the crowd that day, he would have taken one look at me and asked if I liked my supplier and what kind of stuff I got from him. My sheer size got me noticed, and I was asked if I could get drugs all the time. Police officers asked me if I could get them steroids. My answer was always the same: I never sold the stuff, I was just a user. I wore an XXXL T-shirt that fit me tight, and even though my waist was 36 inches, I had to buy pants with a 40-inch waist to accommodate my thighs. I was a beast. I was leg pressing 2,000 pounds with 10 reps.

Moving home was humiliating for me, but I was still focused on one thing and that was to become a professional bodybuilder. I had all of my future hopes pinned on the outcomes of my competitions in 1996. I rationalized that if that meant living at home with my parents so that I could train full time and not work, then so be it.

I think my parents had always known that I had been using steroids, but they just didn't want to admit it. When I moved home, I removed any shadow of doubt. I needed to keep my growth hormone in the refrigerator, so I was forced to tell them. I didn't want them to throw it out; I had spent a lot of money on it.

HGH has to be kept cool. Typically it comes in a powder form along with a solution that is injected into the powder to activate the HGH. It is more expensive than steroids, so I used it wisely. I would do a shot every other day. I couldn't hide that, but I did hide the other drugs I had in the house. I had a whole box of syringes that I'd acquired from a friend of mine who sold medical supplies. When I finished using a syringe, I'd put the cap back on it and get rid of it wherever I could—anywhere other than the kitchen trash can in my parents' house. Seeing a lot of syringes would have made my parents freak.

Having used steroids for years by that point, I began to experience a lot of different problems attributable to steroid use and the massive amount of weight I carried. For starters, I never slept well. Whenever I tried to sleep, I felt like I was suffocating. I remained in a constant state of exhaustion because of my sleeplessness. I also developed a heart murmur. My heart pumped so hard and fast and given the added weight I had on my frame— the human body is just not built to carry that much weight whether it's muscle or fat—and all the drugs pumping through my body, it's a wonder my heart worked at all. I put tremendous strain on my heart.

My mind raced, too. I couldn't shut it down because I felt like if I went to sleep, I wouldn't wake up. It was almost like sleep apnea or something. I was getting an hour or two of sleep a night. I was a wreck. You have to sleep if you want muscle growth, and I wasn't getting any. I'd try to nap on the couch during the day, but it didn't work well. I tried to compensate by going out with some of my friends at night and smoking a lot of marijuana. We'd all get the munchies and then eat so much that I'd be exhausted enough to actually sleep. I was also taking GHB at the time as a supplementary sleep aid. Also known as "the date rape drug," it is commonly used by bodybuilders as an agent to release growth hormones.

I literally couldn't bend over to tie my shoes without straining to breathe. But going to the gym cured everything. It was a sanctuary of mirrors and iron where I felt pumped up all the time.

My stomach became bloated from all of the food I consumed during my bulking-up phase. I still have that bloated look today. People see me and think I have a potbelly, but when I lift up my shirt to show them my abs and they see the development, their jaws drop. Over time, HGH promotes organ growth—the head, hands, and feet.

I also developed gynecomastia—"guyno" or "bitch tits," as body-builders call it. My nipples grew fatty tumors that started to resemble breasts. I had them surgically removed. Fortunately, they weren't cancerous in my case.

In February 1996, I began to start leaning down for the show in May. Once I began to lose the water and fat for the contest, I began to sleep again. I could tie my shoes again, and the murmurs in my heart stopped. My weight dropped from 320 pounds with 22 percent body fat to 259 pounds with 4 percent fat within three months. Once again, I had followed my routine with diet and cardio and leaned down incredibly. Only now I had even more muscle.

I trained hard for the 1996 Mr. California contest. I did a lot of steroids, GHB, and growth hormone for a full year, straight through to the contest. I met Lauren when I was in training. As the contest approached, I started treating Lauren worse and worse. I had so many insecurities about who I was and what I wanted, and all I knew how to do was follow my program: take steroids, diet, and train. I was so jacked up on steroids, booze, and marijuana and put so much hard work and money into the competitions that the pressure finally started getting to me.

But I placed fifth at Contra Costa and sixth in Mr. California out of 20 contestants. While I'd added a bunch of muscle, I wasn't shredded with the same definition that I had shown in previous years. I still retained some water weight. One given in bodybuilding is that the judges are going to nitpick every little part of your body. They don't care how big you are. You have to be so lean and dried up, without any water retention. That's bodybuilding. You learn from your mistakes and correct them for the next year.

I told myself I'd get it done in 1997. But there was another part of me that could not recover from the fact I hadn't done better. Because I derived so much of my identity from bodybuilding, my finish was a devastating blow. I actually thought I would win both contests and stay on the fast track toward becoming a professional bodybuilder. Added to which, my money was about to run out. No money, no steroids or HGH.

Bombing those contests depressed me to no end. Lauren began telling me I should see a doctor and get checked out to see how much physical damage the steroids had done. She and my parents insisted that I get my blood checked. They also wanted me to talk to a doctor about my dependence on steroids. My parents knew I was doing a lot of steroids, and they didn't approve. Even though I'm their son, I was 25 years old, a grown man. I was also stubborn. The good advice from the people who loved me went in one ear and out the other. Mark had expressed his concerns about me to them, too. He told them to keep a close eye on me because of the amount of steroids I was doing. Yet my parents didn't have a clue that I had been supplying Mark with the same stuff that had gotten me into such a mess.

Once depression set in, Lauren and my parents both began to dwell on my steroid usage. They told me my future looked grim if I stayed on them. I wouldn't listen. It was unfortunately in my nature: the more firmly someone asked me to do something, the more likely I would be to do the opposite.

At that point, I shared many of the same qualities as an anorexic person; just at the opposite end of the spectrum. When an anorexic person looks in the mirror, he or she always sees a fat person. There's no such thing as losing enough weight. Even though I was big and strong, I felt like I was weak, small, and a loser. I knew I could get bigger. If I could just push it a little further.… And what I saw in the mirror twisted the picture accordingly. That's how steroids turned on me.

This is where God entered the picture.

While I fought with depression, I did think about the future. But the only future I had ever seen for myself was in bodybuilding. I wanted to compete in 1997. And in order to compete, I needed to do steroids. After a little time off the juice, I was ready to get back on. I still had some leftover drugs, and I planned to use them. I loved to shoot needles into my body because I anticipated the results that were coming. One day, I was standing in the bathroom at my parents' house, about to inject myself in the hip with a needle, and all of a sudden I felt the Holy Spirit of God speak to me, saying that this was going to be the last time I shot up with steroids, or I was going to suffer the cost. *Yeah, right.* Throughout my whole life I had done what I wanted. I didn't have any plans to change.

I went on my way and had a great workout at the gym. I loved taking steroids too much to just quit now. It was the key to my future! But later on that day I started to think about that Voice telling me to stop the drugs or suffer the consequences of health problems and death. It made me stop and think. I felt like I was doing the necessary thing to advance my career and life in bodybuilding. But at that same time, my girlfriend and family worried about me. My parents had told me that I needed to get a job and start making money, that I couldn't just lift weights and live at the house. I began to feel the squeeze from many different directions, and for the first time I began to feel remorse about the person I had become.

Lauren and I were off and on, a typical pattern for me with girlfriends. I treated them all horribly. I pushed them away because I was so insecure. I never felt like they loved me, so I never trusted any of them. I looked to them to always satisfy me, further feeding into my insecurities. I was looking for the love that I needed, but I didn't get it. Who could have loved someone as selfish as I was? As if my horrible, bullying behavior wasn't enough, my mood was constantly fluctuating between high and low. I didn't love myself, so how could I love others?

Everything was all about what Jay wanted and what Jay thought. I didn't think about other people's needs at all. In my mind, if I accomplished things through sports and found success, I felt like I could earn people's love. But I was confusing affection with real love. My girlfriends couldn't love me because they didn't know me. I didn't know myself. I was lost.

Lauren and my family combined forces to stage an intervention. They saw the changes in me for themselves. I felt cornered, like everyone was ganging up on me. I didn't want to go to the doctor because I didn't want to hear a bad report. More important, I didn't want to hear him say that I needed to stop the drugs. But my hand was forced. I broke down and made an appointment.

I got my blood work done and—big surprise—my liver enzymes, cholesterol, and blood pressure were all sky high. They were common side effects of taking steroids. The doctor told me that I was going to have increasingly serious health issues if I didn't get off steroids. The diagnosis brought with it the confirmation from God that the path I had been following would destroy me. I agreed with the doctor that I should discontinue using steroids.

I scheduled a return in a couple of months to get my blood tested again. At the same time, I began seeing a psychiatrist. My depression had to be obvious to him, and I don't know when I've ever felt lower. I had loved the feeling of being on steroids. The power they generated, the euphoria. The notion of not taking them was terrifying. Sure, I'd been through periods when I didn't take steroids—that's what cycling is all about. But never taking them again—ever—well, that felt like losing my best friend.

The doctor put me on an antidepressant drug to combat my obvious depression, a side effect of steroid use. In essence, I went from taking steroids, HGH, alcohol, and marijuana to another drug prescribed by a doctor. The antidepressants were supposed to make me a changed man. I may or may not have been changed, but I can tell you this: I'm not a big fan of antidepressants. Drugs, drugs, and more drugs, that's why so many people are screwed up. The mentality that you can just take a pill and everything will be fine is a line of crap. Of course, I didn't know that at the time. I was under the delusion that I would feel better after popping that little pill. But I was depressed over everything: fighting with Lauren, losing the bodybuilding shows, running out of money and drugs, not having a job, living at home with my parents.... I didn't want to do anything, not even work out. My self-esteem was dwindling. The Incredible Hulk was no more. I felt small and insignificant. I stayed in my bedroom and slept and slept. I was tired all the time. I waited for the antidepressants to work their magic, but every time I woke up I felt worse. I began to ask myself, *When is this drug going to make me feel better about my life?* It never did.

My thoughts even turned to suicide. I didn't want to live anymore. My parents couldn't understand why I wasn't getting any better. After all, I was a strong, able-bodied 26-year-old. Why couldn't I put the old McGwire family work ethic into place and snap out of my funk? I asked myself the same question. Instead, I continued to feel like I wanted to die. *Nobody would miss me*, I thought. I'd turned out to be a loser, the bad apple that spoiled the bunch. And the antidepressants seemed to make everything worse. Instead of making me feel better, they were directing me to deeper, choppier waters.

One night in my bedroom, I found myself overwrought with thoughts about everything, including the unimaginable. I wanted to give up. I began to cry, and once the tears began, I couldn't stop. I asked God to forgive me for my sins. I told Him that I was a sinner. "I give my life to you, Lord," I said. "I'm lost and I'm hurting. Please help and forgive me. I'm done controlling my life and I give it up to You." After I said this prayer, I instantly felt God's presence come over me, from the top of my head all the way through to the bottom of my feet. I felt warm and comforted. A peace ran throughout my body, and for the first time in I don't know how long, I felt hopeful and so secure. It was like nothing I'd ever experienced in my life.

This was the born-again experience I had heard about from the Bible and from converts who described their encounters with God. Sure, I'd heard about "born-again Christians," but I thought it was mumbo jumbo. Now, I was experiencing it firsthand. Goodness, faith, and hope flooded my consciousness. My thoughts instantly changed from death and suicide to life and hope. I understood with great certainty that God would rescue me from the dark corner to which my out-of-control life had taken me. God had waited patiently for me to come to Him. He'd waited until I had totally been broken and there was nothing left of the old me. I had no pride and no selfishness. I understood that I needed to lean on Him, and that He would direct my path by His ways. I had been stubborn, angry, prideful, selfish, living in sexual sin, and doing drugs for most of my life. Now I had found a path out of that life.

After that experience with the Lord that night, I felt so much relief. I woke up the next morning refreshed. I found myself wanting to get out of the house to work out or do something productive. I tossed the antidepressants into the trash.

God began to work on me in mysterious ways. One of my good buddies from childhood, Eric Van Alstine, called me out of the blue. We had worked out together when I was 16. We had been good buddies, even though he's 10 years older than me. We got along well despite our age differences, and he always made me laugh. He invited me to join him at his church in Chino Hills, about 20 minutes away from my parents' house in Claremont. Other than a handful of times when living in the Bay Area, I had only been to a Catholic church. I had gone with my family every week as a kid, and my mentality was that as long as I went, I was a good person. I had that forgiveness card in my back pocket that I could cash in at any time I wanted. That was my safety net no matter what I did. If I partied, had sex, whatever, as long as I went to church and asked for forgiveness, I was okay.

Eric's church wasn't a Catholic church like those in which I had been raised. I remember that first time I went, the pastor started talking about life and scriptures, and something about his preaching totally captured me. It had the same in-your-face truth about Jesus' "Way" that the teachings had when I experienced them at church with Phil Bonadona Jr. back in 1991.

I'm convinced the Lord doesn't want a "religious" relationship from us. That is why my heart didn't move toward Him. I knew of God, from going to church, but I didn't experience Him simply out of religious habit. I believe that God desires a "personal" relationship from us—one on one. And that's why my life changed.

God put Christians in my life, and I started to go to Bible studies. It was invaluable to have people that loved me and helped me through such a tough time. I started to learn God's way by reading and asking questions about His Word of life, the Bible. I had called out to God and prayed for Him to save my life, and He began to do just that by introducing me to more Christians like Eric. God sent these people into my life to get me to quit thinking only about myself.

Soon enough, I began to come out of my funk. Every day I seemed to feel a little better. Every day my emotions seemed to move closer to being under control. I felt a tremendous burden lifted from my shoulders. I'm certain no one could have saved me except for the grace of God. I am convinced of it.

I threw out my remaining drugs, like a chain smoker tossing his carton of Marlboros in the trash. I began listening to my parents and brothers. I also quit supplying Mark. It was over for me. And it was over for him when it was over for me.

The last time I supplied Mark with the stuff was in late April 1996. I drove up to Oakland for the Contra Costa contest. Lauren drove up with me, and she knew something was up with Mark. I never told her about Mark—I never told anyone—but I think she figured it out for herself. I told her the drugs were my stuff for the contest. Other than the supplier/trainer in Sacramento and Walnut Creek, only I knew about Mark using steroids. I lied and denied so easily on Mark's behalf.

My parents were so happy about my turnaround. I told them that it was the Lord Jesus who had saved my life and not the antidepressant pills. I started to learn about life and how God wanted me to live. It was how God worked: He put people like my family, friends, and girlfriends in my life to help me. Lauren, who turned out to be another failed relationship, questioned my use a lot. She just didn't like it. But her influence helped lead me to the place I eventually reached, and I thank her and my family for that.

If I could say anything to people struggling out there, it's that you have to quit thinking about only yourself and live for God. God will take care of you. God will provide for you. And God will bless you for it. I always did what I wanted to do, whenever I wanted to do it. God basically told me that if I was going to do that, He was going to break me down until I fell on my knees and looked up.

chapter | fifteen

The Surge

Mark had gotten what he wanted out of using: he was fully recuperated from his injuries. He could climb the mountain by himself.

Most everybody who believed Mark used steroids assumed he juiced during 1998, his record-breaking season. He has admitted that he dabbled a little bit in '98, but only for a very short time, and to help prevent him from further injury.

Mark seemed relieved that I had put steroids in my rearview mirror. And because he was on such low dosages to begin with, he didn't need the stuff like I did. He had gotten what he wanted out of using: he was fully recuperated from his injuries. He could climb the mountain now. He'd learned the right techniques and requirements for weight training and could do the training by himself. He was on his own. Everything came down to his discipline and lifestyle. Steroids don't give you everything. Using them is simply a shortcut.

After following the program, Mark had adopted his training attitude. He knew what lifestyle he needed to maintain to keep his body strong and healthy. Would he continue to get as big and strong off the stuff as he had on it? No, but Mark had gotten strong enough. Mark simply couldn't afford to keep getting bigger. Besides which, he had been cycling on his hard-core training and drug program mostly during the off-season anyway. In short, I think he was satisfied.

Since I was no longer involved with drugs and supplying Mark, I suggested he start taking more protein supplements or weight gainers to keep up his weight. I also directed him to take "Andro" (androstenedione), a testosterone booster. Andro is nonhormonal. It's not a drug—it was sold over the counter at GNC and other stores. It works naturally with your body, helping you increase your strength and muscle growth. Using Andro had some of the same positive effects that steroids brought, without the negative side effects. It is an herb, a natural hormone enhancer that is a direct precursor to testosterone. When ingested, it elevates the production of your body's own testosterone. In short, Andro will bring out whatever testosterone is in your system. It was what Mark needed to get his own testosterone levels back to normal.

It was perfectly legal in Major League Baseball, and I don't think it was uncommon practice for players to use it, though at the time it was banned from the Olympics. I didn't understand that. My feeling is that whatever is your own testosterone is your own testosterone. Some people's bodies release more testosterone than others', plain and simple.

A part of me wondered if Mark would be the same on the field without steroids, but I also knew he had a great knack for making the necessary adjustments. What he needed was to adjust his confidence level, since the workouts and drugs gave him the lion's share of that confidence. After all, when you feel better about yourself, you're going to perform better. That was how I felt for so many years, and that was the hardest thing to give up. I felt like I couldn't live without it. This was something that I needed. I needed that extra boost to get me where I needed to go.

Mark maintained confidence without steroids because he lived a disciplined lifestyle. You have to credit him for that. He trained hard year-round, ate right, took the right natural supplements, and kept most of his weight and strength by living this way. With that in place, he could get great benefits without drug enhancements.

After my conversion, I felt a lot of remorse about my steroid use. I'd replaced that addiction by letting God into my heart. I had been born again through my Savior, Jesus. My family and friends were all so understanding during this period. Mark supported me during my conversion and seemed genuinely happy about the way I'd turned my life around. Occasionally he called me "Bible thumper," and I know my change probably seemed dramatic. I'm sure it was too much about Jesus for him. But he could see things were going better for me, and that pleased him.

At that point, I didn't know what to do for a living, so out of the blue one day I called L.A. Fitness Sports Club in Diamond Bar and asked the general manager if they were hiring. They were, and he asked me if I had any experience in the fitness industry. "A little bit," I said.

I had been clean for about six months and weighed about 275 pounds with about 12 percent body fat when I walked into L.A. Fitness. I talked with the manager for about five minutes and got hired. I felt so happy to have a job, and I began to sell memberships. I knew how to sell fitness because it was my everything for so long, and I did well.

I could have gotten a job at a lot of different places. But fitness is what I knew, so being in the fitness industry made total sense to me. After God changed my life, I stopped thinking about my own training and started serving others. At first, I still wanted to compete. I felt a twinge at the idea of never competing again. I wrestled with that desire, but little by little, it went away. God took that desire away from me and directed me to other people and pursuits in life.

I still found enjoyment in lifting weights, but now it was in moderation. It's more fulfilling and inspiring motivating other people. The key was to remember that it was for them and not for me anymore. I loved competing, but suddenly those bodybuilding shows for which I had lived didn't seem important to me anymore. Sure, I still wanted to look good and to like what I saw when I looked in the mirror. And being in the gym still felt like a safe haven. Being healthy and staying fit helped me to serve my purpose of inspiring others to want to work hard. You get more attention when you're looking good and feeling good. God used my body, used my size, I think to attract people to me, to give my testimony, and to explain to everyone how God changed my life. I really think that people were inspired by that.

When I first started at L.A. Fitness, I sold memberships and trained on the side. But I noticed that something had changed. When I worked out, I wasn't so into my own world. People would see me lifting and ask me questions. In the past, I would have ignored them. Suddenly, I derived great joy from lending a hand. Pretty soon I had so many people coming up to me to train them that I stopped selling memberships and began paying rent to L.A. Fitness so that I could conduct personal training sessions in the gym full time. Soon after that I got my own apartment in Chino Hills. It felt great to have my own place because I had earned the money to get it.

Everything felt so right. I had finally found my calling. Instead of putting all of my strength and energy into my own body, which I had done for so many years, I directed my attention toward others. I began to live through their results and their attempts to reach their goals. The forging of those relationships gave me a great deal of satisfaction and really served as a blessing for me. Being good at something is important, and fitness was my talent. That pursuit has always brought out the strong desires in my life. Once I peeled away all the layers covering where I'd been, I could see that I had always enjoyed helping others with the use of weight training, way back to those days after school when my friends came over. I loved pushing people to their full potential. By focusing on other people, my life began to change little by little. It gave me drive, purpose, and fulfillment. It's how everyone should live.

I still talked to Mark on the phone all the time. We were still close, but not as close as we were when I'd been living with him. I had changed. I wasn't about partying or women, drinking, or taking drugs. I visited him here and there, but the partying was done. I didn't go out with him anymore. He also had a girlfriend at that time, so he was a little more laid-back.

In 1996, Mark had kicked his game into high gear. He led the major leagues in home runs with 52, becoming only the 14th player in major league history to hit 50 or more home runs. Not only had Mark reached the pinnacle of home-run hitters, he also hit for a huge average at .312 for the season, his career best, if you consider that the only higher average was in 1993 when he hit .333 in 27 games.

Mark missed the first 18 games of the 1996 season because of a foot injury, so when he finished the season with 52 home runs in just 130 games, everybody began to speculate about what Mark could have done in a complete season.

Major League Baseball was still suffering some lingering effects from the 1994 strike, but home runs began to bring people back to the game. Something about the long ball infatuated the fans. Seeing epic blasts like the ones Mark hit was worth the price of admission to many. I'll always believe that executives noticed how much fans craved home runs, and they tried to nurture that craving accordingly—even if it meant looking the other way while the players that played the game began to get bigger and bigger.

What Mark had started in 1996, he continued at the outset of 1997. He had become the most prolific home-run hitter in the game. Then suddenly everybody seemed to be hitting bombs. Attendance grew, and the memory of the strike started to fade away. Of course, in general, players were taking better care of themselves. And serious weight training could definitely transform any Punch-and-Judy hitter into a player capable of hitting bombs—particularly if they concentrated on making improvements in the body's core. But this was something different.

From the outset of the 1997 season, "Big Mac" began to collect homers seemingly on a daily basis. Mark hit 11 homers in April—including an epic 514-foot home run that cleared the roof at Tiger Stadium, making Mark the fourth player to accomplish that feat, along with esteemed company in Harmon Killebrew, Frank Howard, and Cecil Fielder. He added eight in May, 10 in June, and five in July. Unfortunately, Oakland had turned into an also-ran, and they spiraled toward the basement of the American League West. Mark did have some support in the lineup thanks to the presence of a young Jason Giambi and Canseco. But the team was headed nowhere fast, and it became obvious early in the season that the A's would trade Mark.

I think Mark felt a little bit torn about the possibility of a trade, but it certainly didn't affect his performance one iota. He had played his entire career for the A's. They were the team he'd signed with out of USC. The idea of being uprooted started to seem more likely every day. On the other hand, Mark liked the idea of playing meaningful games for a contending team. Once July rolled around, trade rumors had Mark going to any number of places. Finally, on July 31, Major League Baseball's trade deadline, the St. Louis Cardinals traded pitchers T.J. Mathews, Eric Ludwick, and Blake Stein to Oakland in exchange for Mark.

Despite leaving the A's with two months left in the season, Mark still led the team that year in home runs with 34 and tied for the lead in RBIs with 81. He left Oakland as the franchise leader with 363 home runs and 941 RBIs.

Mark felt great about going to the Cardinals since Tony La Russa, his former manager in Oakland, was heading up the team. He knew St. Louis was a great baseball city. He would be playing before big crowds of people who really appreciated baseball. But he never could have foreseen the reception he would get once he arrived in St. Louis. The fans went crazy for him. In his second at-bat at Busch Stadium, Mark hit a 441-foot home run. Not a bad way to get started in front of the hometown fans.

Before the 1997 season had run its course, Mark had four multihomer games, and 24 of his 44 hits with the Cardinals were home runs. On September 16 against the Dodgers, Mark hit a 517-foot homer off the façade above the left-center-field scoreboard, the longest home run ever hit at Busch Stadium. Mark tallied 58 homers for the season. In compiling 50 homers in two consecutive seasons, he joined Babe Ruth as one of the two players in baseball history to accomplish the feat. He also became the first player to hit 20 home runs with two different teams in a season.

Back in California, I watched it all—and I was loving every minute of it. Mark became a superstar and a national icon right before my eyes. I remembered a few years back, sitting with him while his foot was in a cast as he contemplated retirement. Now he was on top of the world, and I had helped him along the way. After the 1997 season, all of the talk in baseball was of the prospect of Mark breaking Roger Maris' single-season home-run record, a chase that had itself basically saved baseball. I felt really proud of him and so did our family. That was a good time for the McGwire family— a really good time.

chapter | sixteen

The Record

Mark's program worked with or without steroids, and his strong work ethic and strict adherence to diet and workout continued to bring him success. He had evolved into a beautifully efficient home-run hitting machine. He was healthier than he had been his entire career.

Mark entered the 1998 season as the face of Major League Baseball.

The Sporting News had named him the 1997 Sportsman of the Year. And his peers in the Major League Baseball Players Association named him their Man of the Year for his leadership and commitment on and off the field. Baseball executives couldn't have gushed over Mark any more than they did. He was their Golden Child. He could do no wrong in their eyes. And in my opinion, he deserved every bit of the recognition he received. He'd worked so hard to accomplish his goals, he had so much God-given talent, and yet he had managed to remain humble.

There was a lot of speculation prior to Mark's trade that whichever team traded for him would be burning a trade, since he was sure to become a free agent at the end of the 1997 season. Everyone knew that he was from Southern California and that he wanted to play there. They couldn't have been more wrong. Instead, he signed a long-term contract that made him the third-highest-paid player in baseball at $8.928 million a year and kept him in St. Louis.

The other players couldn't help but take notice. A player has to be competitive to reach the major leagues and competitive to stay there. Those who thought everybody in baseball was doing steroids had two options: they could either complain about the unfair advantage some players had, or they could get on the juice themselves. I suspect a lot of major leaguers were doing steroids at that time since there was no testing. It was as if the MLB was giving the players its implicit approval. Look at the numbers from those steroid years; even the shortstops and second basemen were putting up 30-plus home runs a year.

I am certain that Mark's performance in those years got a lot of attention from the other players and motivated them to get quicker, faster, stronger, leaner, and bigger—just like Mark. He had added 30 pounds of lean muscle in three years at a slow-enough pace to preserve his flexibility and swing. It was the perfect size for him.

Mark's program worked with or without steroids, and his strong work ethic and strict adherence to diet and workout continued to bring him success. He didn't want to be dependent on the drugs for the rest of his career. Instead he worked hard every day, whether it was during the season or not, and the results continued to be astonishing. My brother had evolved into a beautifully efficient home-run hitting machine. He was healthier than he had been his entire career.

On Opening Day on March 31, 1998, in St. Louis, Mark hit a three-run homer off the Dodgers' Ramon Martinez. It was the first of many home runs in what would become one of baseball's most talked-about seasons.

As the season unfolded, the talk started to center around Mark, Sammy Sosa, and Ken Griffey Jr. chasing Roger Maris' single-season home-run record. All three of them were on a staggering pace to shatter it. Mark seemed to reach a different milestone every day. He hit three home runs against Arizona on April 14 and repeated the feat against the Phillies on May 19. He blasted a 545-foot home run off Florida's Livan Hernandez on May 16. And he became the first player to hit 25 home runs before June 1.

During this time, I continued to work as a personal trainer at L.A. Fitness in Chino Hills. I was feeling really good about myself because I was making good money, paying my bills, and also sharing my testimony with people about how God saved my life. And it was enhanced by watching my brother's successes.

I remember a conversation we had before I went to visit him in St. Louis for the first time. "Jay, a lot has changed," he told me. He wanted to warn me that the media swarmed him wherever he went. I didn't realize the magnitude until I got to St. Louis. The fans were unbelievable. I went in expecting them to act like the people in California who love you when you win and hate you when you lose. But St. Louis fans adored Mark no matter what. Posters of Mark were all over town, and everybody seemed to be wearing jerseys with the number 25. Restaurants covered the tabs, sent wine to the table. Mark and whoever was with him were treated like royalty. People had always been solicitous to him, but this was extreme. He was a national name. Everyone was caught up in the possibility of what he might accomplish. People even approached me for autographs because they could tell by my appearance that I was a McGwire! It was insane. The people in St Louis are really loyal baseball fans who support their home team enthusiastically. They even loved players who didn't play well. In St. Louis, the "boo" was all but taboo.

Considering the circus, Mark handled himself really well. I didn't notice any change in him. He knew that he was doing something special, but he kept proper perspective. He took every day as it came—just another day at the office. Mark remembered 1993 and 1994, and that helped him keep things in perspective. He knew how fast things could change. He was able to enjoy it.

I was impressed by the way he handled the scrutiny. I'd ask him how he could sleep at night knowing that everyone in the world is waiting for him to hit another home run the next day. He'd say, "I just set my mind to it. I keep it simple. I don't worry. I know what I can do. It's all about seeing a good pitch to hit and going out and having fun." And he was able to enjoy the ride. He just had the right attitude. I think a lot of people in the past have crashed under the same kind of pressure Mark faced, and that's why the record had remained untouched.

The attention continued to mount. Things got so crazy that he ultimately hired a bodyguard to accompany him. The guy's name was "Hurricane," and he said he had been a bodyguard for Michael Jordan and other celebrities. On the road when I visited Mark in Houston, the fans were gathered, waiting for him at the hotel. We went through the back entrance, and the fans still found a way to get to him, clamoring for autographs, pictures…everyone wanted a piece of him. The next morning, the fans were still there waiting.

At the park in Houston, the announcer barked, "Now batting, number 25, Mark McGwire," and the Astros fans went crazy, giving him a standing ovation. It was that incredible. The opposing team's fans were rooting for Mark to hit a bomb. The whole country was behind him. They all wanted to see baseball history in the making.

Throughout that season, he continued to do all the things that had gotten him to that point. He did eye exercises, he stretched to remain loose, and he understood the fuel he put into his body. If Mark went to a restaurant, he would know how much protein each entrée contained. Knowing the protein count allowed him to make smart choices.

He also supplemented his diet with Androstenedione. His use of the stuff caused a ruckus in 1998, despite the fact that it was an over-the-counter supplement. Mark's understanding of the substance was simple: it's legal. He kept the Andro in his locker, in plain sight. Late that summer, an Associated Press reporter noticed a bottle in Mark's locker and splashed headlines across the nation. How could a Major League Baseball player use such a strong performance-enhancing substance? he crowed. The NFL, the International Olympic Committee, and the NCAA all had a ban on Andro. Of course, Major League Baseball did not. It was character assassination, plain and simple. Mark was following the letter of the law, but his integrity was put on trial in the court of public opinion.

In the aftermath of the story, many came to Mark's defense. Some berated the reporter for snooping, and others looked at the discovery as proof that Mark was using legal supplements and not steroids. After all, why mess with Andro if you were using more potent real stuff? Androstendione doesn't even come close to steroids. Facts are facts: one is a drug, the other is not.

Tony La Russa, who was a lawyer before pursuing baseball full time, believed Mark's right to privacy had been violated and that the Associated Press needed to be taken to task for the violation. The Cardinals organization put out an official statement supporting their beloved slugger's use of the substance that read in part, "[Androstenedione] has no proven anabolic effects nor significant side effects.... Due to current research that lacks any documentary evidence of any adverse side effects, the Cardinals' medical staff cannot object to Mark's choice to use this legal over-the-counter supplement."

Baseball commissioner Bud Selig and union chief Don Fehr also weighed in on the matter. Selig called the Cardinals a "disciplined organization" and surmised, "I don't think anything goes on there that shouldn't." Fehr commented that Andro was not regulated by the FDA and could be purchased over the counter, concluding, "It seems inappropriate that such [press] reports should overshadow the accomplishments of players such as Mark McGwire."

Many players lined up in Mark's defense, too. Even sportswriters rallied for his cause.

Baseball was quick to admonish the reporter and sweep it under the rug. Stories about Andro and suggestions that Mark's home runs were coming by virtue of anything other than skill were not to be tolerated. After all, the home-run chase was such a great feel-good story. Mark McGwire, the All-American boy, chasing the sport's most hallowed record. And Sammy Sosa, the vibrant outfielder of the Chicago Cubs, was pacing Mark along the way. Reams of copy were being produced daily detailing this pursuit. It was saving baseball! Why would anybody try to ruin that?

A simple look at the McGwire family tree would have opened the eyes of most reporters if they cared to look. I was a bodybuilder—and I had never hid the fact I did steroids. I freely admitted it. Had a reporter done a little background search on Mark, he would have found that he had a kid brother who had crashed on steroids. Anybody with half a brain would have uncovered that the same kid brother had helped Mark train, that he lived in his house for a time—that same time when Mark's health improved drastically and he piled on 30 pounds of muscle—and that maybe, just maybe, he might have introduced Mark to steroids.

I dreaded the thought of a reporter confronting me with questions. I wouldn't lie, but I didn't want to expose the truth, either, in protecting Mark.

The moment never came. Rick Reilly of *Sports Illustrated* was the only journalist who ever tried to reach out to me. I didn't return his call, and he never tried again. Later I read Reilly's story, and it mentioned that I had once been on steroids and had trained Mark, but Reilly never suggested that Mark had ever used anything stronger than Andro.

And so the magic summer of 1998 marched on.

By the middle of August, Griffey had sustained injuries that took him out of the race. But Mark and Sosa were still going strong. The pair seized the moment, and it was a superb race to the finish. On August 19, Sosa went ahead in the race when he hit his 48th home run. Then Mark answered back later that day with two home runs to give him 49 and regain the lead.

What made the story even more compelling was the fledgling friendship between the two. Mark liked Sammy. He considered him a funny and humble guy and a slugger with great ability.

Mark included his son, Matt, in the excitement that summer. Because of the divorce and as a professional baseball player who was on the road for the better part of the year, he never had been able to spend as much time with him as he had wanted. Matt lived in Orange County with his mother. Kathy never stood in the way of Mark seeing Matt, but logistics prevented him from being around. Their relationship was as good as it could be for someone who was always on the road. During the off-season, Mark went out of his way to spend time with Matt. So seeing Matt spending time with his father during that exciting summer was nice and gratifying for me, as his uncle.

On September 8, the two home-run kings came face to face as the Cubs came to St. Louis. Mark had already tied the record, hitting his 61st home run on our father's 61st birthday—an incredibly special birthday present to him. Everybody in America was tuned in to their televisions to see if the record-breaking home run would come that night.

I didn't make the trip to St. Louis. There was no guarantee that he would hit one in that game, or the next, so I figured I had to lead my life and train my clients. I might not have been in St. Louis, but I was just as excited when Mark came up to bat as I would have been if I had been there. I was standing around the free-weights area, and everybody yelled, "Your brother's up, your brother's up." Everyone was on pins and needles waiting to see if it would happen. Steve Trachsel was on the mound for the Cubs. and at approximately 7:18 PM, Mark swung and hit what appeared to be a screaming line drive. Jack Buck had the call:

"Down the left-field line, is it enough? Gone! There it is! Sixty-two! Touch first, Mark. You are the new single-season home-run king!"

It was incredible. Everybody in the gym knew that Mark was my brother, and we were all going nuts. Everybody gave me hugs and told me how awesome they thought Mark was. I saw my parents and my brother Dan on TV. The crowd at Busch Stadium went nuts. Members of Roger Maris' family were on hand to watch history made, as well. And since the Cardinals were playing the Cubs, Sosa was there to congratulate Mark. And I think all of those moments between Mark and Sammy were genuine and awesome—especially this one. They respected each other and understood what the other was going through. The stadium worker who found the ball handed it over free of charge to Mark. It was an incredible moment.

After Mark set the record—which, by the way, he did in 145 games— Sammy didn't just disappear. In fact, a lot of people wondered if Mark would hang on to win the home-run title. How ironic would that have been if Mark had broken Maris' record only to lose it again by the end of the season? Sammy tied Mark at 62, and then they went back and forth until the last weekend of the season. In the end, Mark finished with a flourish, hitting four home runs the last weekend of the season for a total of 70 home runs, four ahead of Sammy's 66.

Mark got the home-run record, but Sosa won the National League's Most Valuable Player Award after helping the Cubs reach the playoffs. Even so, the *Sporting News* named Mark the co-winner of their Sportsman of the Year Award (with Sosa), *Sports Illustrated* named him their Sportsman of the

Year, and the Associated Press named him the Player of the Year, among just a few accolades. And through it all, Mark remained as humble as ever.

That off-season Mark bought me a '98 Ford Explorer. I needed new wheels because my car was breaking down a lot. I believe this was Mark's way of saying thank you for being a part of his success. I had helped him save his career by getting him into the right lifestyle and helping him to heal by prescribing the right stuff for him.

Not only did that 1998 season save the game of baseball, but Mark became a recognizable face worldwide. Following the 1998 season, Mark took a trip to Australia. He sat down at a table in the back of a quiet restaurant. When he stood up to leave, everybody in the restaurant began to clap for him. Somewhat taken aback, Mark waved to the room and left.

chapter | seventeen

The Exit

Mark exhausted multiple rehab assignments, but nothing worked. So, after hitting 29 homers in 97 games in 2001, Mark decided it was time to retire. He told me baseball just wasn't fun anymore.

Mark had reached the pinnacle of his popularity and success in 1998. Everybody wanted a piece of my brother—the sportswriters, the fans, and advertisers clamoring to have "Big Mac" endorse their products. With his red hair and freckles, Mark had the All-American boy look. He was a household name. Who wouldn't want Mark on board?

Miraculously, Mark followed his record-breaking season with an almost equally astounding season in 1999, hitting 65 home runs. Nobody in baseball could ever stake claim to 135 home runs in two consecutive seasons. He made it look easy. Every homer seemed to travel 400 feet or more. They all just sailed.

He continued hitting home runs at an amazing pace—slamming more than 30 before the All-Star break in 2000—but the effects of tendonitis in his right knee began to take their toll. The back leg is essential for any hitter if he wants to turn on a baseball—it's the area of the body that provides the necessary power to put baseballs into the cheap seats. And Mark had been giving it a heck of a workout. Every time he swung, the pain alarm went off. Had he still been using Deca, he could have avoided the injury. But he hadn't been, and by the end of the season, the Cardinals were in the playoffs, but Mark was a pinch-hitter.

Mark exhausted multiple rehab assignments, but nothing worked. The aggravation he experienced extinguished whatever joy he might have found in playing. Going to the ballpark became a chore. So, after hitting 29 homers in 97 games in 2001, Mark decided it was time to retire. He told me baseball just wasn't fun anymore.

The fans in St. Louis loved him, as did the Cardinals organization. The team offered him $30 million to stay on for two more years, but he basically told them that they should give it to someone else. And sure enough, that's when Albert Pujols arrived.

If he could have remained healthy, there's no telling how many more home runs he could have hit in his career. But he was 37, he'd made plenty of money—and taken care of most of it—and he'd never really enjoyed being in the spotlight. In hindsight, I think all of the attention he got in 1997 and 1998 really burned him out. I think it turned a quiet man into a recluse.

Mark had one heck of a run. From 1995 to 2001, he hit 345 home runs, incredible by any stretch but especially considering he spent so much of his career battling injuries. Just think what a healthy Mark McGwire might have done! There's no doubt in my mind that he would have blazed past Henry Aaron's career home-run mark. He could have been untouchable.

True to his word, he had remained unmarried throughout his career. Once out of baseball, he got remarried and began working on a new life. He shrunk from the spotlight, as secluded as DiMaggio.

Meanwhile, I had been doing my own thing since my conversion, and basically I was a happy guy. But I hadn't formed any meaningful romantic relationships. I accepted that—I felt that God wanted me to mature before I was able to contribute to a relationship. I was still insecure, but I was gaining self-confidence. I found fulfillment in helping others, both through personal training and from sharing my experiences and how I had grown from them. I could see that people looked at me with real respect—for maybe the first time in my life.

It was a great time in my life, and I grew a lot as a person, but I found myself to longing for a soul mate. I wanted a wife and a family. My buddy Rock suggested that I make a list of all the qualities I was searching for in a spouse. His suggestion sounded kind of odd to me, but I proceeded to do just that. By the time I had finished, I had a list of 22 desirable traits. I felt if I were fortunate enough to find a woman with many of these traits, I would truly be blessed. And he said that I should pray every day for the wife that I sought.

Approximately one year later, another friend approached me. His name was Rocky San Angelo. (I know, two Rockys for friends—funny.) He wanted to introduce me to a one of his kickboxing students. I had noticed her before—I trained clients at the gym during the same hour as the class—and I found her attractive. I agreed, and he set us up on a more-or-less blind date. To my amazement, she fulfilled 20 of the 22 desirable traits that I had put on my list. As far as I was concerned, I had wound up with two perfect 10s.

Francine and I now have three wonderful children. Eric is her son from a previous marriage, but I feel like he is one of my own. And Francine and I have two little girls, McKenzie and Brooke—the two cutest girls in the world, in my wildly biased opinion. Francine's parents, Fred and Irene DiGiorgio, are wonderful people, too. Irene keeps me well fed whenever she's around, and Fred is a wonderful advisor in business and personal matters alike. Fatherhood has been everything I hoped it would be. I feel blessed to have a family so full of love.

Unfortunately, protecting my own family resulted in a rift with my brother. Mark and his then-fiancé came over to see our new home in early 2002. Given the long and rocky road I had traveled to get to this point, I was excited to have my family together and show them my first home. The afternoon had been everything I hoped it would be. Everyone was having a great time. Laughter rang through the home. Then suddenly things took a drastic turn for the worse.

Francine and I were in the kitchen talking with Mark. My stepson Eric and my nephew John came running into the kitchen. As he passed by, Eric tickled Mark, causing Mark to spill coffee on himself. Just like that, Mark went off. He took it upon himself to discipline Eric, swatting him right on the backside. You could have heard a pin drop in the room after that. No one knew how to react. Francine seemed so stunned that her jaw literally dropped. Someone needed to speak up, so I told Mark that disciplining Eric was our job as parents, not his.

Since that day, Mark has not attended one of our family's events. Francine was so hurt that she even refused to attend Mark's wedding. In fairness to Mark, he apologized after the fact. But things were never the same after that. Not attending the wedding only drove us further apart. My wife and I have made attempts to reach out to Mark since then, but I've been met with failure. My family has intervened, and I asked my parents and my brother Bob to tell Mark that we wanted to make contact. Mark told Bob that he would call us sometime. Three years later, we're still waiting for that call. I still love my brother. I think Mark is hurt that we didn't go to his wedding. I know most families are dysfunctional, but I think it comes down to forgiveness. I hope we get there.

Mark's a cool customer when it comes to shutting down, but I never expected that he would shut down on me. Over the years, he's been a great brother, and we were really close for a time. He's a very giving and compassionate person, but I think he's hardened his heart over the years.

* * *

When the House Government Reform Committee subpoenaed several players and baseball executives to testify regarding steroids on national TV, we brothers were not there to support Mark, though I would have liked to have been. But I can guarantee Mark was shocked by his subpoena. Personally, I thought the whole thing was a dog-and-pony show. Surely there are more productive things our government could have been doing besides chasing the ghost of steroids past. Major League Baseball should have handled it, but they never did, so the government had to get involved.

It had been a long time since I had talked to Mark, so I had no idea what his approach would be when he was called before Congress. His day came on March 17, 2005. Watching him take a seat, I was nervous. Would they rake him over the coals? Would politicians grandstand at his expense? As it turned out, he didn't say much. Mark is and always has been a private person. His business was his business, and he didn't stick his nose in anyone else's.

Mark had not made a public appearance in years, so the sight of him shocked a lot of people. They remembered "Big Mac," the thick-muscled slugger who led the famous charge on Roger Maris' home-run record. Taking the stand in 2005, he looked more like the old Mark McGwire.

Players Sammy Sosa and Rafael Palmeiro denied under oath that they had not used steroids, but Mark didn't offer a denial or confirmation. Congressman William Clay from Missouri asked Mark whether he could tell fans that he had played the game with honesty and integrity, to which Mark replied: "I'm not going to go into the past or talk about my past. I'm here to make a positive influence on this."

He also refused to defend himself against Jose Canseco's allegations that the two of them had used steroids together. Instead he told the panel that his lawyers had advised him not to answer those questions because they could jeopardize his friends, family, and himself. For my part, I would not have cared; I would have told the truth and been done with it.

Mark did concede that baseball had experienced a problem with steroid use, and he offered to help lawmakers find a way for younger players to fight the temptation of using performance-enhancing drugs.

I think that pleading the fifth was the wrong way to go, that he had some bad advice from his attorneys. I had hoped he would confess, though my parents had told me that he would probably plead the fifth. Even though we'd had a falling out, I felt for Mark—and he took a beating that day. Had he just taken the same route as Jason Giambi or Andy Pettitte, both of whom admitted their guilt and offered apologies, I suspect nobody would be worried about what he did today. But that wasn't Mark.

Sadly, it's the way he has dealt with things throughout his life—don't talk about it, and it will go away—and how he's dealing with it today. His legacy is tarnished as a result. And that's a shame.

Epilogue

On January 11, 2010, Mark officially admitted to using steroids. The news hit baseball like a thunderbolt. Suddenly, the whispers of *Did he or didn't he?* stopped.

Mark didn't lie in his admission, but he didn't tell the whole story.

He expressed his regrets for playing in baseball's steroids era, an insinuation that the culture of steroids was pervasive in Major League Baseball. And in truth, I think that everybody should take a little bit of the heat and responsibility for what happened at that time—the players, the owners, the trainers (like me), the media, and even the fans.

The fans and the media lust for greatness, and that puts pressure on athletes day in and day out to perform at the highest level. They want to see records busted open; they want size, strength, and endurance—superheroes making the impossible possible. And Mark was one of those heroes, plain and simple.

I remember once when Mark hit a home run at Dodger Stadium. Legendary broadcaster Vin Scully said it was one of the longest home runs he had ever seen hit. The ball bounced off the roof in left-center field and into the parking lot. The next day I heard a fan on the radio talking about it. He had been walking to his car when Mark hit that bomb and said the ball had bounced past him and hit another car before he grabbed it. He didn't know Mark had hit the ball until everyone around him told him. He assumed someone had thrown a ball in the parking lot. And why would he have thought otherwise? Mark made the impossible possible.

Turning their backs on the obvious, the owners saw more and more tickets sold. People were coming back to the ballpark. Baseball was back again. Everybody made money. The Players Union didn't want to make a push to ban steroids. So instead it became the only way to remain competitive. Besides, as the strike had shown, there were countless players out there willing to step in—players who might not have problems using steroids if it meant making it to the major leagues.

Who knows what might have happened if I didn't start Mark on a program. Maybe he wouldn't have made it back to baseball at all. And maybe players like Rafael Palmeiro, Alex Rodriguez, and Barry Bonds (as many have suspected) wouldn't have ever gotten involved with the stuff, either. If Mark hadn't been getting all the glory and hitting all those home runs, would Bonds have gotten on the sauce? I think Mark's success had an effect on the rest of the players in the league.

Commissioner Selig said it himself: the steroid era is over. But is it?

* * *

The question remains: *What will be the legacy of Mark McGwire?*

Baseball's "asterisk" system is untenable. There is no way to determine who it affects and who it doesn't. We will never know. Moreover, where does one draw a line in the gray area of "competitive advantage"? How can anyone say that players A, B, C, and D used while players E, F, G, and H did not? Baseball has recently turned its nose up at steroids and the way they changed the game. If they want to preach about the possible health problems associated with steroid usage, I'm all for it. But as far as making all of these players live at the foot of the cross for having used steroids, I'm vehemently against it on a couple of different levels.

My brother was faced with a difficult decision: Should I use so I can get healthy and remain in the major leagues or should I take my chances without using? I think any player in that era would have made the same decision. Speaking for myself in my twenties, I know my answer. For a chance at baseball immortality as well as a chance at the big bucks, I would have said yes in a heartbeat. These were men who had known nothing but baseball their entire lives. Many of them signed right out of high school. They needed to remain in the major leagues to make a living. Steroids were a runaway train in baseball—and you were either aboard or you weren't.

Earl Weaver, the former Hall of Fame manager of the Baltimore Orioles, was asked whether he was embarrassed by the steroids era. He said, "Oh, I don't know. Not really. You're always looking for an edge. And guys, that's their living. And if a growth hormone helps you to be better physically and able to do more things physically...but it just shatters the records."

Before steroids, the "edge" was something else. Decades before, players grabbed a handful of "greenies" before they took the field. Greenies were benignly known in baseball circles as pep pills, though in reality they were amphetamines, or speed.

Hall of Fame pitcher Gaylord Perry won 314 games and two Cy Young Awards in his 22 major league seasons. In his 1974 memoir, *Me and the Spitter*, Perry enumerates the dozens of ways in which he doctored the ball—from lubricants to other on-the-mound hijinks—in order to render the ball unhittable.

Plenty of ballplayers abused alcohol or drugs, many times in plain sight of their coaches and managers. Many of those guys are in Cooperstown today. I'm not advocating cheating in baseball, or smoking marijuana, or using speed or steroids. I'm just saying that baseball's moral compass seems to shift as it best suits the sport.

Looking at today's game, it's hard not to be suspicious of some of the sluggers out there. HGH is still available, and the tests to detect it are very expensive. And even then, they aren't particularly effective. If I was a betting man, I'd wager that HGH is prevalent in the major leagues and other sports today. For players who rely on that paycheck, that strength, that size, that power for their careers, how could it not be? Athletes are going to do whatever it takes to succeed at the professional level.

Even so, taking the shortcut of steroids is just that: a shortcut and a way to stay healthy. Without real skill, a player will get nowhere. In Mark's case, it was his innate ability to hit the ball—something he had demonstrated time and again throughout his career—that got the home run crown. Former Yankees manager Ralph Houk told ESPN, "I think [McGwire] broke [Maris'] record fairly. I wouldn't be concerned about it. [McGwire] was a good hitter that deserves everything he's got." I believe Houk is right. For whatever advantage Mark may have gotten from steroids, his achievement speaks for itself. Mark was, and always will be, a superlative hitter.

The difference in Mark's game wasn't just the muscle mass he gained from steroids, it was the discipline, the strength, and the endurance that he gained from *the program*. By 1996 Mark already had the body, the mindset, and the plan to make it all work. I'm convinced that his further use in '98 wasn't about getting big—it was about remaining well.

* * *

It's been eight years since the last time I talked to my brother. It's hard to believe how quickly that time passes. For my part, I needed to give my testimony, to tell the true story about what really went on, from what happened with Mark to how steroids nearly killed me and how God saved my life. But I do believe that the truth is powerful and that the record should show what really happened. Mark himself acknowledged that the weight of this secret had taken its toll on him. I believe that the truth will set us both free.

Now that he has come clean, I believe that the fans will forgive him. In the long term, they will respect him because they can now understand his motivation. And after all, isn't he the one who brought baseball back from the brink?

*　　*　　*

I have not touched steroids in 14 years. I am totally natural now, but I've managed to keep most of my size—I weigh about 265 nowadays. I kept my physique because I work hard at it.

I still lift like a bodybuilder because I love it, but it's a hobby now and not an addiction. Without steroids, building the body the way you want it to be is more of a complex puzzle. But I'll never forget that steroids are just a shortcut. You still have to bust your butt in the gym to get where you want to get. And more importantly, it's a costly shortcut—one that nearly cost me my life.

God has put me in a place where I can put my knowledge and experience toward helping others. I'm training people and passing on the blessings of being in good shape to others. I now own my own gym, and I've trained hundreds upon hundreds of people over the years. Being able to make a difference in someone's life has come to be my life's purpose. I've taken my accumulated knowledge and experience in weight training and nutrition—and how to do it safely and healthily—and I am passing it on. Working with others has been better than bodybuilding. I wish I'd known it sooner.

I'm now an advocate against steroids in competition, even in bodybuilding competition. I advise clients that the natural way is the only way, and I write up good nutritional programs and get them on some good power movements that will change their bodies naturally. I've done a complete turnaround from where I was 14 years ago. I feel rewarded every day.

People who take steroids for too long or who have taken too many know all too well the consequences of the drug. Jose Canseco talked about it at length in a documentary about his life. I can relate to his trials.

Steroids need to be out of sports and society completely. They hurt people physically and emotionally. They are incredibly addictive and debilitating. On them, you begin to believe you can't accomplish anything on your own. They make you feel that with them, you can't fail. I felt so great while using them that I never wanted to get off them. It was a vicious cycle.

Steroids create depression and mood swings. They kill your liver. They harm your heart and circulation with high blood pressure and increased cholesterol levels. Steroids upset the body's hormonal balance and kill your sex drive. What starts as an innocent way to be "competitive" can end up being fatal. It's not the kind of "edge" an athlete wants.

For years, I have been caught between telling the truth and being loyal to Mark. For years, I chose Mark, even after he cut off communication with me. My hope is that in revealing this story, I can help change someone else's. Now, the truth is out there. And if my testimony helps educate someone else about the dangers of taking steroids, if one or more people choose to not take these drugs, then all of this has been worth it.